AF751665

MIDNIGHT MURDER AT HAMLINGTON HALL

BY MARK KILMURRY AND JAMIE OXENBOULD

CURRENCY PRESS
The performing arts publisher

ENSEMBLE THEATRE

CURRENT THEATRE SERIES

First published in 2023
by Currency Press
Gadigal Land, Suite 310, 46–56 Kippax Street, Surry Hills, NSW 2010, Australia
enquiries@currency.com.au
www.currency.com.au

in association with Ensemble Theatre

Reprinted 2025.

Typeset by Brighton Gray for Currency Press.
Printed by Fineline Print + Copy Services, Revesby, NSW.
Cover image shows Jamie Oxenbould. Cover image by Richard Hedger.
Cover design by Alphabet Studio.

Currency Press acknowledges the Traditional Owners of the Country on which we live and work. We pay our respects to all Aboriginal and Torres Strait Islander Elders, past and present.

NATIONAL LIBRARY OF AUSTRALIA

A catalogue record for this book is available from the National Library of Australia

Contents

Midnight Murder at Hamlington Hall was first produced by Ensemble Theatre, Cammeraigal Country, Kirribilli, on 1 December 2023, with the following cast:

SHANE	Sam O'Sullivan
BARNEY	Jamie Oxenbould
KAREN	Ariadne Sgouros
PHILLIPA	Eloise Snape

Director, Mark Kilmurry
Assistant Director, Emma Canalese
Set and Costume Designer, Simon Greer
Lighting Designer, Verity Hampson
Composer and Sound Designer, Daryl Wallis
Stage Manager, Erin Shaw
Assistant Stage Manager, Christopher Starnawski
Special Observer, Toby Blome
Costume Supervisor, Sara Kolijn

CHARACTERS

KAREN
PHILLIPA
SHANE
BARNEY
RICHARD

ROLES IN THE PLAY

MARGARET MATHEWSON, nurse, nursed the parson in his final months (*played by Karen*)

MADAME ESMERELDA, a clairvoyant (*played by Karen*)

MRS GLORIA WHITTINGTON, actress, a favourite of the parson (*played by Phillipa*)

INGRID, a seafarer (*played by Phillipa*)

LADY SMYTHE, a local society matron (*played by Phillipa*)

BENSON, butler (*played by Barney*)

GILES, farmer who runs Hamlington Estate (*played by Barney*)

TAFFY HEMINGWAY, playboy, distant relation to the parson (*played by Barney*)

COLONEL MUNSTER, served with the parson in the Air Force (*played by Barney*)

ERNEST BLACK, detective, enjoyed playing murder-mystery games with the parson (*played by Shane*)

MR BARTON, the parson's solicitor (*played by Richard*)

DOCTOR *Freddie Pennington-Ermington* (*played by Richard in Scenes One and Three, Barney in Scene Two, Shane in Scenes Five and Six*)

MAID (*played by no-one*)

This play text went to press before the end of rehearsals and may differ from the play as performed.

The setting is a community hall/theatre space somewhere on the North Shore. Home of many community groups, including the Middling Cove Players—an amateur dramatic society that has been going for many years.

Tonight is the opening night of their new play—Midnight Murder at Hamlington Hall.

An empty stage. PHILLIPA*—in all the Lululemon exercise gear—brings a yoga mat on and starts to warm up. She is in her thirties and is very keen. She does a lot of 'red leather, yellow leather', 'lion face GRRRR, lemon face OOOO', and warms up continuously through* KAREN*'s lines.*

KAREN, *the stage manager, comes down stairs from the bio box. She is pragmatic and a little dry. But still excited for opening night.*

KAREN: Hi, Phillipa, first one in as usual.

PHILLIPA: Well, opening night! I like to be extra warmed up. Steaming. Piping hot!

KAREN: I know, you're—

PHILLIPA: I actually start my warm-up routine about eleven a.m. Get the body moving. The voice humming. I focus the whole day on tuning the instrument.

KAREN: Don't you work?

PHILLIPA: God no! Opening nights I always take two or three days off in the lead-up.

KAREN: Lucky you.

PHILLIPA: [*oblivious*] I know, my manager's great about it, and the office can do without me for a few days. Well they can't. There'll be a shit-ton of fires to put out when I get back but … anyway, not tonight.

KAREN: Absolutely. Is there anything you need?

PHILLIPA: I'm all good.

KAREN: Well, just yell.

PHILLIPA: [*condescending*] You've got enough to do, Karen. You're the real star, I just wish you got to feel all that love us actors do.

KAREN: I'm fine, really.

PHILLIPA: You're the best. Did you manage to fix those speakers? There's still a hum.

KAREN: I joined a few wires together. Fingers crossed.

SHANE *enters with flowers and a gift.*

SHANE *is the director of the show (and the MC Players). He is enthusiastic and a born optimist—though tonight he has the weight of the world on his shoulders. He has dedicated his life to am-dram.*

SHANE: Good evening! I just saw Tim in the foyer, we are completely full tonight! Like a …

He struggles for a metaphor.

Ripe Stilton cheese, tonight is about to go OFF!

KAREN: Evening, Shane. Is that a saying?

SHANE: Probably not. Evening, Karen … everything okay? No catastrophes?

KAREN: Not yet … but the night is young.

KAREN *continues her set-up.* PHILLIPA *continues to warm up.*

PHILLIPA: Hi, Shane. Who are they for?

SHANE: The whole company! An opening-night dressing room just feels empty without flowers.

PHILLIPA: Oh thank you. You're a doll.

SHANE: A doll … [*Trying to be funny*] not a ventriloquist dummy I hope …

PHILLIPA: No …

SHANE: Hand up the— Or a sex doll??

PHILLIPA: No …

SHANE: Dolly … Parton! … sorry, I don't know what that was. I'm a little anxious … [*Re the flowers*] Umm, just a little chookas … and thank you … and congratulations.

PHILLIPA: What for?

SHANE: I was going through the records today—slow day at the bank—and I realised, this is your tenth show with the Middling Cove Players. For you.

He gives her a gift. A collage of photos in a frame.

PHILLIPA: Ten! Wow. [*Re gift*] Oh it's beautiful. A collage of all my roles.

SHANE: Took me hours. From your first production of *Funny Girl* when you gave us your Fanny … Brice.

PHILLIPA: I was awful.

SHANE: Nonsense, I loved your Fanny … Brice … you were a star even then. *Cabaret* …

PHILLIPA: Stop it.

SHANE: What did the *North Shore Times* say?

PHILLIPA: [*too quickly*] 'Brave and daring' … I think, I don't know …

SHANE: And her doubling as the Nazi Officer was both 'troubling yet sexy'.

PHILLIPA: It was wasn't it?

SHANE: Your Esmerelda in *Quasimodo*!

PHILLIPA: Now that was a show! Your Quasimodo was just … oh …

SHANE: Remember you made me carry you to rehearsals—

SHANE / PHILLIPA: —'Cause that's what he would've done.

PHILLIPA: Till you did your back in.

SHANE: Had to do the show in a brace in the end. Still, made the hunch quite realistic …

PHILLIPA: [*touched by the gift*] Thank you … this is very special.

SHANE: Well you know how much you mean to me … and the Middling Cove Players.

PHILLIPA *acknowledges his feelings.*

SHANE: Anyway, enough about past triumphs. Here's to tonight's triumph! Chookas to us.

PHILLIPA: Chookas to us.

TOGETHER: Toi toi toi!

SHANE *is a ball of suppressed terror, but his optimism and 'never say die' attitude overcomes it.*

SHANE: I am never more alive than just before an opening. I feel like I've got a mixture of coffee, Red Bull and Gatorade coursing through my veins. Which I probably do, 'cause that's all I've had since yesterday.

KAREN *enters.*

KAREN: Shane, bit of a problem backstage, the karate classes left it like a pigsty. There's vomit in the boys' dressing room and, I'm sorry, I do not do boy vomit.

SHANE: Leave it to me. Won't be the first time I've cleaned up a bit of backstage vom. Remember when Doug Hancock played Stanley in *Streetcar* a few productions ago?

PHILLIPA: Oh God don't remind me.

SHANE: Poor man exploded from both ends with nerves. Backstage was like a Jackson Pollock painting.

PHILLIPA: You know one night his eyes actually bled when he yelled 'Stella'.

SHANE: Well, the stage is not for everyone.

KAREN *leaves.*

PHILLIPA: He is an excellent periodontist though. My mum still goes to him.

SHANE: How is Janice? Is she coming tonight?

PHILLIPA: [*a painful subject*] I think she'll be here. It's her Book Club night, so who knows. Typical. And I think Damian's coming.

SHANE: [*wounded*] Damian? I thought that was all off.

PHILLIPA: I'm giving him one last chance.

SHANE: Oh Pip … After that whole aquarobics debacle.

PHILLIPA: He said he was in the changing rooms looking for me.

SHANE: In the showers?

PHILLIPA: He said he was sweaty … he'd been bike riding … Anyway I can't go into this now, I need a clear head.

SHANE: Of course, of course, let's shake it off.

They shake it off.

We'll pop that in a balloon … and let it go.

He mimes it out. She's a terrible mime.

Gone. But your mum's coming. That's nice. I like your mum.

PHILLIPA: Do you? She doesn't go in for the theatre much. Thinks it's all a bit … silly.

SHANE: SILLY!! Of course it's silly. That's why we do it. A bit of silliness to distract us from life! Someone famous said that once. Or maybe I just did … who knows? Anyhoo … you keep warming up. I'll drop these in the 'room of green', clean the karate-class mess, then join you.

He gives her another, slightly too long, hug.

Tonight's going to be perfect.

PHILLIPA: You betcha.

Just before he leaves …

SHANE: [*quietly to* PHILLIPA—*nervous*] Do you think Karen's going to be okay? She seems a bit more annoyed than usual.

PHILLIPA: That's just her. She's fine.

SHANE: Is it weird she chose to do her community service with us? … She kind of scares me a li—

Just then KAREN *enters and scares* SHANE.

Yeeeaaa … oookay yes, Karen, it's … look … hello … Vomit. On it.

He goes backstage.

PHILLIPA *continues to warm up. Weird stretches and vocal exercises.*

KAREN: He was talking about me wasn't he?

PHILLIPA: Hmm? No … maybe, I don't know. I think he ummm just wondered … why … you chose here to serve your sentence?

KAREN: 'Serve my sentence'? It's not like community service with you lot is hard time. Plus it's better than picking up rubbish … just.

PHILLIPA: Good for you. Gets in your blood doesn't it? And I don't care what you did … little bit of fraud or if you killed someone??

Trying to get out of her what crime she committed.

KAREN: I did not kill anyone, Phillipa … yet.

PHILLIPA: Okay. Sure. Hey when you get a moment can you check my blouse, I think I lost a button.

KAREN: When I get a moment? Sure. I'm just fixing some broken props, then I have to get the sound desk to work otherwise we won't have any sound effects tonight, rig the special, iron all the costumes … then I'll get onto that button.

PHILLIPA: [*oblivious*] Thank you! And I'd love a green tea if you're passing the bar.

KAREN *starts to leave.*

I'd give you a hand … but this— [*Indicating her voice and body*] won't warm up by itself.

KAREN: Of course. You're our star.

PHILLIPA: Oh shush, I wouldn't say 'star' … I can't stop other people saying it though.

KAREN *leaves.* BARNEY *enters from foyer.*

He is the old guard of the MC Players. Very theatrical. Lives for the theatre.

BARNEY: [*singing*] Another opening … another show!! Aah, Phillipa, look at you, first one in to warm up. First one in, last one out. Like the marines! A woman after my own heart. I played a marine once. *South Pacific*, right here on this stage. He wasn't actually a marine, just a seaman (not that kind), but in my mind he was a marine. [*Singing*] 'There is nothin' like a dame!!' You know I sang 'nothin' like a DANE' that whole show. Thought it was some pro-Scandi thing. How are you feeling lovey?

He burps.

Excuse I m'darling, just had a very decent pub dinner … [*Whispering*] and a cheeky Shiraz, don't tell Herr Director …

PHILLIPA: I'm ready to go.

BARNEY: Course you are. Course you are! We're kindred spirits, Pippi Longbottom! Greasepaint in our blood.

He spreads his arms wide and takes a big sniff.

Smell that?

PHILLIPA: Is it the mess from the karate class?

BARNEY: It's the smell of an opening night. It's the smell of expectation, nerves, passion and piss all rolled into one. Peter Brook knew it. Kenny Branagh knew it … Darryl Somers knew it. I'd bottle it if I could. 'Opening' … by Calvin Klein.

He's on stage by now. He takes off his coat, does one small stretch. Loudly sings some opera, coughs, then ...

Yep, all there. I'm warmed up and ready to go. Oh, little note, are you choosing to play Ingrid lopsided?

PHILLIPA: Lopsided?

BARNEY: Seemed a little crooked in the dress. Remember! … Posture … up, up, up. Stance forty-five degrees. Little hop when you enter, little hop when you exit. And always look at whoever's talking. Right AT them.

Points to her, then to some imaginary character.

Don't look at THEM … unless you're thinking about them … then just a quick glance … then bang … back to THEM. It's simple stuff.

As he starts to swan offstage, SHANE *enters.*

PHILLIPA *is now concerned about her posture. And her stance.*

Evening, Shane.

SHANE: Evening, Barney … excited?

BARNEY: Any more and I'd get arrested!! [*Exiting*] Oh and two words love … Camel and toe.

PHILLIPA *gives* BARNEY *the finger as he leaves. She adjusts her warm-up gear.*

SHANE *is on stage in his pre-show warm-up outfit. Perhaps a leotard.*

SHANE: I didn't notice anything.

PHILLIPA: He's giving me notes now. Me!!

SHANE: Right … that's no good. Anything you want to go over?

PHILLIPA: Actually the reunion scene I'd love to look at when Con gets here. I don't think I really nailed it in the dress-up rehearsal.

SHANE: Really? I thought it was all there. Con's the one who needs to work on it.

PHILLIPA: Well, I didn't want to say anything. I know how much you've got on your plate … directing, acting and writing this one. I feel like I haven't quite cracked the scene yet … Con can be a bit … closed off, emotionally.

SHANE: I thought it might be 'cause he has a little bit of a crush on you.

PHILLIPA: [*disingenuous*] On me! Don't be silly. No he just hates his wife that's all. He's only here because it keeps him out of the house.

SHANE: I mean he'd be silly not to. Anyway … let's run through it. See if I can help. That's my job.

They run through part of the scene where they discover they are a long-lost couple.

PHILLIPA*'s acting is enchantingly earnest.* SHANE *is better, but completely caught up in the moment of being this intimate with* PHILLIPA.

Let's remember our intimacy training.

PHILLIPA: Of course. Always ask before you do anything.

They take a breath and start the scene.

DOCTOR (SHANE): Oh good heavens!! Look here …

He shows her his ring.

INGRID (PHILLIPA): [*gasps dramatically*] They're identical!!

DOCTOR: These were our betrothal rings … Rebecca?? … It can't be! … (Is it okay if I put my hand here?) But your pale alabaster skin and auburn hair??

INGRID: Sunkissed after years at sea … (Is it okay if I move a little closer?) and hair bleached blonde by the cruel Mediterranean sun.

DOCTOR: Rebecca. Oh my darling Becky.

INGRID: But I have no memory of a husband—of any life before the shipwreck! … (Is it okay if I touch your hair?) But the rings … it's irrefutable … hang on …

She tries different ways of saying the line.

But the rings, it's irrefutable?? … No hang on … But the rings? It's. IRRRREFUTABLE! That's it.

DOCTOR: Allow me to take you in my arms. Perhaps the closeness of our hearts will reignite our passion.

They awkwardly start to get closer and closer. It starts to build to a climax.

INGRID: Doctor, I—

DOCTOR: Sssshhh … (Here okay?)

INGRID: Please.

DOCTOR: There?

INGRID: Yes. Do you mind if I … ?

DOCTOR: Of course … Is this … ?

INGRID: Absolutely.

By now they are in each other's arms.

Oh Freddie …

DOCTOR: Oh Rebecca …

They stop just before the kiss.

BOTH: And scene.

PHILLIPA: That was … see, I was relaxed. Felt honest.

SHANE: [*excited*] I felt it too.

PHILLIPA: If only Con could give me that.

SHANE: I'd be happy if he just stopped flailing his arms in the air every time he spoke. Nearly took my eye out in the dress.

PHILLIPA: He wears a dress?

SHANE: Dress rehearsal.

PHILLIPA *looks quizzical.*

Dress-*up* rehearsal.

PHILLIPA: Aah yes.

SHANE: But … it's nice to have some new blood in the company.

KAREN *enters.*

KAREN: Shane. Sorry to interrupt … Umm, bit of bad news. Pam and Percy Begg just called. They weren't feeling well, so they thought they'd do a test before they came in … and, they're both positive.

PHILLIPA / SHANE: Fuck it!! / You're kidding me!

KAREN: Pam was so apologetic. They're both just gutted, said they shouldn't have gone to that Fondue Festival … but obviously they won't be coming in tonight.

PHILLIPA *starts to get panicky and potty-mouthed.*

PHILLIPA: Fondue fuckers!! Sorry.

SHANE *paces and figures it out.*

SHANE: Let me think …

KAREN: I'm really sorry guys.

SHANE: For what?

KAREN: Well, shouldn't we cancel, or postpone tonight?

PHILLIPA: I knew it was all going too well. Something had to go wrong …

SHANE: Phillipa, breathe, it's okay …

PHILLIPA: First Damian flashing everyone at the pool, then my mum making fun of my acting, now the fucking Beggs … sorry.

SHANE: [*working it out*] Phillipa … it's fine, of course we're not cancelling. Heindrich can play the Doctor and Helen can play Gloria. It'll be fine. It'll work, trust me. The show must go on.

Pause.

KAREN: Why?

SHANE: It just … must. That's showbiz. It's what we do.

BARNEY *enters in his bathrobe.*

BARNEY: What's all this? Showbiz talk, without me? Of course the show must go on, what's happened?

KAREN: Percy and Pam have the lurgy. They're not coming.

SHANE: It's fine. Heindrich can play the Doctor and Helen can do Gloria.

BARNEY: Heindrich—play the Doctor! You can't be serious, Shane? Let me play the Doc, I can do it on my ear.

SHANE: I know you can, Barney … and can you close the bathrobe a little …

BARNEY: Come, come. We're all artists here!!

KAREN: Don't you work at Harvey Norman?

BARNEY: I manage small appliances … it can be artistic! … What happened to freedom of expression??

KAREN: Pretty sure that didn't mean having to look at middle-aged balls.

BARNEY: Heindrich hardly speaks English. He doesn't know what he's saying half the time. He said 'shall we tire of the drawing room' in the dress … up. Luckily I stepped in with some impro and saved the day.

SHANE: Barney, listen, there are too many scenes with the Colonel and the Doctor. It would be impossible.

BARNEY: You saw my one-man show—if anyone in our troupe can play two characters in one scene it's me. (Six is my record.)

SHANE: Trust me, this will work best.

BARNEY: You're the boss.

SHANE: Just over two hours to showtime. We'll do a quick walk-through when Heindrich and Helen get here. Karen, if you could make the necessary adjustments to costume thank you.

KAREN: Sure. By the way, the sound desk is still on the blink.

SHANE: Have you tried—

KAREN: Kicking it? Yes, several times.

BARNEY: It always comes good. It has an actor's temperament. Doctor Theatre always does the trick.

KAREN: My niece is staying with me—she's up there with the manual seeing what she can do.

They all wave up to the bio box.

SHANE: You've got yourself an assistant, great. Her generation have a way with … gadgets.

Sound comes on way too loud—

KAREN: Please don't touch anything.

—then lowers. KAREN *leaves, talking to her niece on her headset.*

But that's really helpful thanks.

PHILLIPA: [*flustered*] Alright, I'm going to steam my make-up for a few minutes and start my voice. I mean … you know what I mean.

PHILLIPA *leaves.*

BARNEY: Glad we've got a moment before the cyclone hits. Before I put on my slap, Shane, can I have a word?

SHANE: If it's to pitch 'Blarney with Barney' to me again, can we just get tonight over with mate?

BARNEY: Of course, of course, let's put that on the back burner for now. No—what I wanted to say was … two years you've been at the top job here at the Middling Cove Players, and since you've taken over from Doreen, which couldn't have been easy, you have done a sterling job young man. And yes, I was overlooked for succession … but, well, if it was going to be anyone else, I'm glad it's you … And tonight … writing, directing and acting!

SHANE: Producing, designing, dramaturgy, publicity—

BARNEY: YES … it's a tour de forza … as they say in … the classics.

SHANE: Thanks, Barney …

BARNEY: And just let me plant a little seed for next year's *Wizard of Oz* …

SHANE: Well the Wizard's already cast.

BARNEY: No … Dorothy.

SHANE: Er—

BARNEY: 'I guess we're not in Kansas anymore' …

SHANE *is speechless.*

Think about it. Anyway … from the old guard, what I wanted to say was … chookas for tonight lovey. Big hug!

SHANE: Thanks, Barney. Coming from you, a founding member, that's—

BARNEY: Only one left. God I remember those early days. Dirty Dicks would let us use their space on Monday and Tuesday when they were closed. That first year, it must have been … '82 … we did *Henry V* and *Move Over Mrs Markham* in rep. I played Full-stuff and the flamboyant interior decorator.

SHANE: I think it's pronounced Falstaff.

BARNEY: Common misconception. If you read the First Folio I think you'll find it's … [*In 'Olde English'*] Feouull-stuff. And it's actually Prince Hoool.

Googie taught me that.

Pause.

That's Withers. Googie Withers.

SHANE: I know, Barn.

BARNEY: One of my mentors … I played her love interest at Marian Street back in the day.

SHANE: Well … understudied.

BARNEY: And then Doreen talked the council into making the community centre our permanent home, and here we still are. You at the helm … producing NEW work … so exciting.

SHANE: It is isn't it? And I feel we owe it to Mable Shtint to make it work.

BARNEY: Mable—??

SHANE: Shtint. She wrote the novel that I adapted the play from.

BARNEY: Oh yes, I meant to read it but the shop's been busy—end-of-year sales.

SHANE: *Midnight Murder* was her eighty-ninth novel I think. Mostly self-published—but some were quite good. Critics called her a 'fourth-rate Agatha Christie'.

BARNEY: Ouch.

SHANE: I know right?! In my mind she's at least third—and possibly even second-rate!! But I think I've been faithful to the Shtint Legacy. And if it goes well … I'm hoping we might give it a push to a professional company.

BARNEY: Imagine that! A pro company putting on our work—your work. Actually getting PAID to do this funny old business we call show.

SHANE: Well I guess that's the dream. Not that there's anything wrong with am-dram of course.

BARNEY: Of course.

SHANE: Always for the love—not the money.

BARNEY: Always. I was that close you know. To going pro. Gaden had my career. Jammy bastard.

SHANE: Now, Barney, keep this to yourself, but as a founder you should know. The council are in tonight. Apparently they're making a decision about if we should still have the hall or not.

BARNEY: What?!

SHANE: They want to give the space to some fitness company.

BARNEY: No!

SHANE: There's money in making people sweat.

BARNEY: We sweat! Actors sweat! I'm sweating now!!

He open his robe to prove it.

They can't do that! We're an institution in Middling Cove!

SHANE: Maybe. But we've got to prove we can put on top-shelf work or it's no space and no funding.

BARNEY: All our work is top-shelf. As good as anything on the main stages.

SHANE: Oh I know.

BARNEY: Classic bureaucratic dream-crushers. I've seen it before, Doreen always managed to put them off somehow … I think she 'knew' the mayor, if you know what I mean.

SHANE: We need to impress them tonight, Barney.

BARNEY: [*deadly serious*] Oh we will my friend. We … WIIIILL!! See, that's acting.

PHILLIPA *re-enters with an an inhaler and a very red-based foundation. Still warming up loudly.*

Pip darling. Little heavy on the slap?

PHILLIPA: What do you mean?

BARNEY: That's a lot of Max Factor Red you've got on …

PHILLIPA: Ingrid's spent half her life outdoors on the sea, it says in the script her 'skin is rosier and hair blonder from the sun'.

BARNEY: Was there a solarium on the boat?

SHANE: Could be a tad too much.

BARNEY: A tad? She's a shade off having first-degree burns.

PHILLIPA: Shane said 'push the boat out' in terms of character.

SHANE: I did … but—

PHILLIPA: I wasn't allowed to do the 'Mediterranean' accent.

SHANE: [*diplomatically*] Well I'm just not sure what that is exactly.

PHILLIPA: And I'm not sure I've really nailed her voice yet.

SHANE: No it's fine, Pip … Ingrid's our love interest, she just needs to be a natural … beautiful soul, like you.

PHILLIPA: Now I'm blushing.

BARNEY: You wouldn't know.

SHANE: She's less outdoorsy—more—lovable, cockney girl-next-doorsy.

PHILLIPA: Next door to who?

SHANE: Everyone. She's everyone's 'girl next door'.

PHILLIPA: Girl next door eh.

She thinks deeply.

Hmmmm—I did live next door to someone. And I am a girl. Okay, great, thanks, Shane, I can work with that.

SHANE: Brilliant. Breakthrough moment?!

They high-five.

PHILLIPA: You always know the right thing to say.

BARNEY: That's the director's job. Well, the good ones. And Shane's a good one. I don't care what a few of our members are saying …

KAREN *enters in a panic.*

KAREN: Barney … robe. Shane, I just got a call from Helen. She and Heindrich and Con have all got it too.

PHILLIPA: Motherfuckers!

BARNEY: All three of them?

KAREN: Apparently they all went to a Pilates class together and the instructor had it.

PHILLIPA: [*quietly to* SHANE] I think they're in a thrupple.

SHANE: Oh God … And they've all done tests?

KAREN: They just got their PCRs confirmed. They want to know what they should do.

SHANE: Well obviously they can't come in. Council protocol.

KAREN: And I phoned Marcia, 'cause I know she's immuno-compromised …

PHILLIPA: Oh boo hoo Marcia.

KAREN: … and she wants to play it safe. She's staying home too.

SHANE: Oh God …

PHILLIPA: [*incensed*] What the fuck were they doing at Pilates? What happened to our bubble?

KAREN: People still have to live their lives.

PHILLIPA: Do they?

BARNEY: Not everyone's as committed to the cause as us, Phillipa. You'll learn that when you've been around as long as I have.

SHANE: Okay … okay … let me think.

KAREN: What is there to think about? We have to cancel now. Also … is anyone going to ask if they're feeling okay?

Pause.

SHANE / OTHERS: Oh … are they feeling okay?

KAREN: I don't know! I didn't ask! Shall I let the box office know?

SHANE: No!! Nobody move. Let me think …

Long pause. He does some mental calculations. He paces and plays out the play in his head. A Beautiful Mind *moment.*

BARNEY *tells a 'knock knock' joke quietly in the silence.* SHANE *looks at him.*

BARNEY: Just trying to lighten the mood.

SHANE: We can still do this.

KAREN: What??

SHANE: Put the damn show on, what do you think!! Excuse my language.

BARNEY: That's the spirit!!

KAREN: Shane … I don't think there's—

PHILLIPA: How? There's three actors standing—we have thirteen characters!

SHANE: We are not cancelling!! We've worked too long and hard on this to just throw up our hands. The show MUST go on.

KAREN: Why? I never really got a good explanation. Why must the show go on? Is it a legal thing? Will we be fined by the Amateur Dramatic Society Police Force?

BARNEY: We have our own force?

PHILLIPA: Shane, this means as much to me as it does to you, but I don't want to compromise the play—

SHANE: With all due respect, Pip, I don't think it does mean as much to you—or anyone. I found this book in a second-hand store when I was holidaying in Scotland … just after Sharon dumped me—

ALL: You told us this story. / We know. / We've heard this …

SHANE: LET ME FINISH!! … And when I read it … I said to myself … Shane—you are not going to go down an emotional rabbit hole just because your fiancée left you for her exotic-looking sexy Spanish guitar teacher … NO! … You are going to turn this masterpiece into a STAGE PLAY, and make it the best damn night of murder mystery thrills and spills that the Middling Cove Players' audience has EVER SEEN. And I bloody well did that!! In my lunchtimes and slow periods at the bank I toiled away—

BARNEY: [*getting caught up in the story*] Quill in hand …

They all look at him.

Not a quill … but … you know … that's the vibe I was getting … just … carry on …

SHANE: And now here we are after months of rehearsing, giving up our evenings, our weekends, our relationships!

PHILLIPA: … occasionally our Tuesday lunchtimes …

SHANE: … and for what … ??

KAREN: What?

BARNEY: For the fucking love of our craft dammit!! This hallowed space … this church of—!! … Sorry go on, Shane.

SHANE: To just say 'sorry audience'— (who are already gathering out there in the foyer) 'but we are going to disappoint you I'm afraid. Sorry you had an expensive schnitzel at the pub, booked a babysitter, finally got a park—but you're just going to have to go home and watch *Survivor*!!'

KAREN: Why can't we just say, nature has defeated us … we'll put our show on when we aren't all suffering from some rampant virus.

SHANE: I DONT KNOW WHY OKAY?! The SHOW … MUST … GO … ON. That's what the saying is. The show goes on … regardless.

BARNEY: They have those sayings for a reason, Karen!

SHANE: We've only got a five-night season. It's tonight or never.

PHILLIPA: [*getting caught up in* SHANE*'s enthusiasm*] Yes … yes … I hear you, Shane, I do. But I have enough stress doing one character, let alone two.

BARNEY: Two!! … Child's play! Why not three or four? This is the chance of a lifetime, now grab it!

SHANE: Do you want to be showing some poor schmuck around a three-bedroom bungalow in Balgowlah on Monday and suddenly realise you passed up this chance to show an audience your versatility! … Your real talent? Je ne regrette rien!

BARNEY: Ooh, I love Italian.

KAREN: This is just madness.

PHILLIPA: [*buying in to the idea now*] What … Mad like Lear? Or Blanche De—Boyce?? … If that's madness, then bring it on baby!!

SHANE: There's my star!!

PHILLIPA: I am literally fizzing with opening-night energy! If I was any more warmed up I'd be cooked. I'm with you, Shane, a hundred and fifty-seven percent!

BARNEY: Oddly specific.

KAREN: [*still perplexed*] Why put yourselves through this? You're not even getting paid … it'll be chaos.

BARNEY: Because we love it, lovey! It's our calling.

SHANE: Thank you, Barney. I know it sounds mad, Karen, but we're actors dammit—

KAREN: Amateur actors … and technically I'm not—

SHANE: I'm including stage managers in that, Karen! … We're actors and stage managers dammit … and actors and stage managers can do anything!

He searches for an inspiring quote.

To infinity … and beyond!!

KAREN: *Toy Story*?

SHANE: I was going for an inspirational quote … that's all that came.

PHILLIPA: Totally worked.

SHANE: I'm not saying this is going to be easy. It's going to be a struggle. But did Zelensky give up when the going got tough??

KAREN: Did he just—

SHANE: Did Oscar Wilde give up when they threw him in jail for his art??

KAREN: [*quietly*] He did actually.

SHANE: Did the cast of *Neighbours* give up when they were repeatedly told by various networks that their show was cancelled?? No, they picked themselves up, regrouped and carried on. And look at them now.

BARNEY: Still plugging away.

SHANE: Now somebody get me a whiteboard. I have a plan.

No-one moves. Eventually KAREN *realises it's her who's going to have to get the whiteboard.*

Lights out. Lights up and they are gathered around a whiteboard with an elaborate plan of who will play who. Lots of lists, names crossed out, arrows, etc.

They are all talking at once, pointing to the board, etc. SHANE *is crossing out and writing in various permutations of the cast list.*

It's like a war-room situation.

Finally ...

Okay … So … Phillipa, you'll play Ingrid as rehearsed, as well as Gloria and Lady Smythe.

PHILLIPA: Right. Gloria—I should be fine with. She's a famous actress … hmmm … [*Thinking*] I'll give her some Cate Blanchett vibes … icy and aloof.

SHANE: More *Blue Jasmine*. Less *Lord of the Rings*.

BARNEY: Different ears.

SHANE: Just think big. She's a diva.

KAREN: [*to* BARNEY] I think she's got that down.

PHILLIPA: Lady Smythe— I won't be able to mimic Mrs Faadeema's accent exactly.

KAREN: [*firmly*] She's not doing the accent!

BARNEY: Karen's right. Anything east of Romania is out of bounds accent-wise. Trust me, I've got the reviews to prove it. They crucified my 'Gandhi'.

PHILLIPA: [*in terrible Scandi accent*] How about a Scandi accent?

SHANE: NO!! … No … no Scandi … Make it your own. Do your standard English accent. Just go for something more upper-class, Maggie Smith *Downton Abbey*-ish.

PHILLIPA: Oh I can do that. Love that show.

She does her best Maggie Smith.

'There's nothing simpler than avoiding people you don't like. Avoiding one's friends, that's the real test.'

BARNEY: Maggie Smith … not Dick Smith.

SHANE: Barney … you'll play the Colonel as rehearsed … as well as Benson the butler, Taffy, Giles and the Doctor in Scene Two.

BARNEY: Is that all? I can do more.

SHANE: [*humouring him*] Jump in if we miss anything. You're our veteran.

BARNEY: And my impro skills … Benson should work well for that. The others I'll switch up accents, maybe a limp or a stutter … God I feel so alive!

SHANE: Karen … you're the only other one who knows the play. I need you to play Nurse Margaret and Madame Esmerelda.

KAREN: Me? Act??

PHILLIPA: Ooh, you get to wear the sparkly cloak and act mysterious.

BARNEY: Is that what that was?

KAREN: A: the cloak is the size of a tent. B: who will work the sound and lights? And C: why don't we just—

ALL: We are not cancelling!

SHANE: Karen, please, I'm begging you. I know you can do this. I realise this is not what you thought you'd be doing when you agreed to do your … hours here at the Players.

BARNEY: Your what?

SHANE: [*trying to be sensitive*] Karen is doing her community service hours here with us … we thought it—

BARNEY: A criminal amongst us! How exotic. It's like Jean Genet … or Jim McNeil!!

They look at him blankly.

Google them!

KAREN: If I say yes … what about the lights?

SHANE: Your niece. The cues are all written in the prompt copy, she just has to follow along.

KAREN: She's twelve!

They all look up to the bio box, from where comes a voice (maybe our real stage manager?).

NIECE: It should be fine. I think I've figured it out.

The stage suddenly goes to black.

Okay. Not that button.

Lights come back on.

Got it!

SHANE: See! She'll be fine.

KAREN: Aah, what the hell. I'll do it. But I want you to fudge my hours and give me a shit-hot reference when we're done.

SHANE: Consider it fudged.

KAREN: Fine, I'll get the cloak.

PHILLIPA: What about you?

SHANE: Well, I'll do Detective Black as rehearsed. But mainly I'll just try and steer things along—keep the ship going forward so to speak.

PHILLIPA: And the Doctor in Scene Five … ?

SHANE: That's the …

PHILLIPA: … reconciliation scene. You were so good just before, makes sense if you do it …

SHANE: That does make the most sense. Hopefully I can feel … the feelings.

BARNEY: [*pointing to whiteboard*] What about this? Question mark against the Solicitor and Doctor in Scene One and Three.

SHANE: Leave that to me. I've got a plan.

KAREN: So if multiple people are playing the Doctor, won't that be confusing?

SHANE: Not at all. Just make sure whenever you're the Doctor, you carry the medical bag.

PHILLIPA: What about name tags? I've got some.

SHANE: If you think it'll help.

BARNEY: You know, when I performed with Googie at—

PHILLIPA / SHANE: Understudied.

BARNEY: I went on for a matinee!

KAREN: [*to* SHANE] What about the maid?

PHILLIPA: The shitting maid!!

SHANE: Just look offstage whenever you refer to her. If she has a line, someone chime in.

PHILLIPA: Fuck that's bastard clever.

KAREN: Good. I never liked seeing Marcia in that maid's outfit.

BARNEY: Really? I thought it worked …

SHANE: Now, Barney, as the butler … a couple of things …

KAREN: I'll just nip up and … call my parole officer.

They all look at her. It's a strange thing to say.

She winks and laughs.

Kidding. ACTING. I mean it's just lying isn't it.

SHANE: Bit more to it than that …

KAREN: Meh …

KAREN *goes up to the bio box.*

BARNEY: [*whispering*] What do you think she did?

SHANE: Did?

BARNEY: What was her crime? My guess is violence was involved.

SHANE: Don't ask … just don't make her angry.

SHANE: [*quietly to* PHILLIPA, *indicating Karen*] Be ready to step in if that all goes to buggery.

PHILLIPA: I can always sing if things go wrong. I've got one ready to go … give us time to get back on track.

She starts to sing 'Don't Rain On My Parade'. SHANE *cuts her off.*

SHANE: Hopefully it won't come to that.

PHILLIPA: Don't worry, Shane, I was born to sing.

SHANE: So, Barney … the butler … please, for the love of God, don't leave the suitcases in the entrance like Percy kept doing.

He's grabbed a suitcase from the props table.

Put them here. Not here. They've got to be out of the way.

BARNEY: Yes, of course Shano. Not my first rodeo. Put them here, not here …

He puts them in the wrong spot.

SHANE: No, there! … Not there!

He puts them in the right spot.

BARNEY: There, not there. Locked in. Now with Benson … I thought, a touch of James Mason. I do a good Mason. Benign … but something untrustworthy bubbling under the surface.

SHANE: Nice I like it. Like in *Lolita* maybe … ?

BARNEY: I was thinking more *Salem's Lot*. But good note.

SHANE: Never mind. James Mason is a good touchstone.

BARNEY: [*exiting*] Okay, I need a walk for Giles …

He starts to leave, sipping his hip flask as he goes.

Maybe a wooden leg … perhaps he lost it in a thresher accident back in '39 …

PHILLIPA: You've given him four extra characters to play—you're not worried about him blanking?

SHANE: He has the odd dry, true … but he's a trouper, he'll be fine.

PHILLIPA: And the robe? I can't have another *Les Mis* incident.

SHANE: I know. I know.

PHILLIPA: Courgette was my dream role and he ruined it for me!

SHANE: For everyone.

PHILLIPA: What possessed him to do 'One Day More' in the nude?

SHANE: It was only one night … and he only takes his clothes off when he panics.

They both shiver at the mental image.

Now, Gloria and Lady Smythe. You think you know them?

PHILLIPA: Oh I know them. I know all your characters. They're so beautifully drawn.

SHANE: I meant, do you know the lines?

PHILLIPA: Oh God yes.

SHANE: You really are my rock. [*Taking her hand*] Thank you. I know I can harp on about the story and how much the theatre means to me blah blah blah … but it's also about the … friendships … and our crazy little community.

PHILLIPA: You're right you know. What we do here is important. I'm going to call my mum and Damian and tell them not to bother coming. I don't need that negativity.

SHANE: Okay.

PHILLIPA: We're going to be fucking amazing tonight. And I don't want to share that with anyone else.

PHILLIPA *leaves.* SHANE *punches the air and throws his shoulder out.*

For a moment he is alone on stage, with the book and script in his hands. He takes a moment to convince himself ...

SHANE: You got this.

KAREN *enters.*

Oh, Karen, can we please just run through that tricky Esmerelda bit in Scene Four?

KAREN: Umm, sure.

SHANE: From … 'These are all police matters' …

ESMERELDA (KAREN): These are all police matters of which you lot—

She has immediately nailed an Eastern European accent and acts quite well.

SHANE: [*surprised*] Oh.

KAREN: What? Didn't think I'd be any good?

SHANE: Not at all … that's … exactly how I always imagined her. Keep going.

ESMERELDA: … police matters of which you lot had no answer and turned to me for help. All of which I assisted in solving.

DETECTIVE (SHANE): Impressive Esmerelda.

ESMERELDA: Thank you.

DETECTIVE: Not at all.

ESMERELDA: Then I look forward …

DETECTIVE: To what exactly?

ESMERELDA: Exactly.

DETECTIVE: Precisely.

ESMERELDA: Elementary.

DETECTIVE: Thank you.

ESMERELDA: Not at all.

SHANE: No we end on 'Thank you'. That bit starts with 'Impressive' and ends with 'Thank you'.

KAREN: Got it.

SHANE: Don't want to end up going in circles.

KAREN: No worries. Now, on to bigger issues. I've spoken to my niece, she's nervous, but she's going to do it.

SHANE: Yess!

KAREN: Lights are okay … I think. She's fixed the sound effects somehow … the music she's Bluetooth-ing off her phone or something, I didn't really listen …

SHANE: Good for her … another Middling Cove Stage Manager in the making.

KAREN: Not happening.

SHANE: Oh, and Karen, what ever happens, don't forget to turn on the camera for Hamlington's speech.

KAREN: Do we need to do it live? It's going to be a problem.

SHANE: Yes!! All the pro companies have live cameras in their shows. It's a thing.

PHILLIPA *re-enters.*

PHILLIPA: Just a thought on Gloria. Scene One, when we first meet her, what if SHE'S singing?

SHANE: Singing? Why would she be—

PHILLIPA: Well, she's a famous actress, they're always singing.

SHANE: Are they?

KAREN: Name one?

PHILLIPA: Gwyneth Paltrow.

KAREN *groans.*

Her bone broth is very good.

KAREN: You want to sing don't you, Phillipa?

PHILLIPA: Nooooo. Well, I mean. I could.

SHANE: But we agreed you're going to sing if something goes wrong.

PHILLIPA: What if nothing goes wrong?

KAREN: Ha!

BARNEY *enters in a bad wig.*

BARNEY: Shano. Found this toupée in the costume room. It's a bit musty, but I thought … Taffy!

SHANE: It's not exactly—

KAREN: Is it on backwards?

PHILLIPA: Oh, I can smell it from here.

BARNEY: I think it works.

SHANE: Go for it, Barney. If it works for you …

BARNEY: Yes!

SHANE: 'If *you* feel it—then the *character* feels it.' Someone said that.

BARNEY: Probably Stan-Zelensky

KAREN: You mean Stanislavsky?

BARNEY: I know my –nskys, Karen! I'm an outside–in actor … I work from the facial hair—in.

KAREN: I think that toupée will do a lot of the heavy lifting, Barney.

BARNEY: I could raid my false-teeth box.

SHANE: Ahhhh … just make him … louder … maybe?

BARNEY: Louder. Yes. Brilliant. And the teeth. Oooh you're good, Shane. That's why they pay you the big bucks.

SHANE: Ha. Imagine getting paid to do this.

The actors all look at each other.

ALL: Ha! / As if. / Be nice wouldn't it? [*etc.*]

SHANE: One last thing. We'll have a safe word …

BARNEY: Good idea, I use them a lot.

SHANE: If things really go off the rails and we need to discuss something without the audience knowing … just say the safe word and we'll convene under the portrait.

KAREN: What's the safe word?

BARNEY: Mine's 'Ouch' … which doesn't always work.

PHILLIPA: Pineapple!

KAREN: Amsterdam!

They all call out some ridiculous words at once.

ALL: Cuttlefish! / Boob tube! / Werewolf! / Backgammon! / Help! / Help me!

SHANE: No, it has to feel like it's part of the play. Just say 'I'm parched'.

They all agree. Good choice.

Okay, come together team.

He gathers them in a circle.

Now, we've got this, right?

KAREN: Is that a question?

SHANE: [*more confidently*] Sorry. No. We've got this—right.

BARNEY: Course we do. Have faith. And those council bastards will love it.

PHILLIPA: What does that mean?

BARNEY: Oops, sorry mate.

PHILLIPA: What's he talking about, Shane?

SHANE: [*serious*] It's nothing … look … I didn't want to worry you all—but the council's here … watching, and … kind of deciding the company's fate tonight.

PHILLIPA: Motherfuckers. Sorry … it's P.I.P.M.

KAREN: What?

PHILLIPA: Panic-Induced Potty Mouth.

KAREN: Right.

SHANE: Budget cuts.

BARNEY: You're right they are a bunch of—

SHANE: We're expendable, the arts always are …

BARNEY: They want to turn it into some sort of sweatshop??

SHANE: It's all fine. If we just give them a good old show … like we always do … they'll see what we do is worth hanging on to.

KAREN: Want me to make a call? I know some people who—

SHANE: NO! No … we just go on with the show … be amazing … and cross our fingers. And remember, Golden Rule … we NEVER GO OFF-SCRIPT.

BARNEY: Weeeell …

SHANE: Never, Barney!

KAREN: And remember Jenny Caccielli's party will start dead on ten next door. And having seen those speakers arrive, it's going to be loud.

SHANE: If nothing goes wrong, we'll be done by then.

He takes a big breath. Delivers his heroic speech.

Now … we … all of us here at the Middling Cove Players … are storytellers. We are part of a tradition of showfolk. Tonight we face adversity. But we will not take a backwards step. It won't be easy. Good art. True art—never is. But tonight is our night dammit … our opening night. And by thy hook or thy crook … the show …

ALL: WILL … GO … ON!!

Upbeat music transition.

All of them madly get the stage ready for the show.

They push the last bits of furniture into place. Final props, etc.

Some acting/rehearsal business between BARNEY, PHILLIPA *and* KAREN.

Then lights go down and a spot comes up on SHANE *entering, in costume.*

He does the curtain speech.

Thank you and welcome to opening night of the Middling Cove Players' world premiere of *Midnight Murder at Hamlington Hall.*

Applause.

Firstly I'd like to welcome our distinguished guests—Mr Mayor and our local member, Fiona … something, sorry I've just drawn a blank.

And our sponsors who are also here I think—Pat and Darrel Hannity of Hannity Meats—

We see the sponsors' logos and photos on the screen.

'For all your meat and small goods needs.' And long-time sponsors Pink Flower Funerals—'You'll be dying to see us.' Thanks for your support.

I see a few of our members, past and present, of the MC Players. Gerry, thanks for helping with the set—I know it can't be easy from the wheelchair. Hope the knee gets better. Bev and Joan for all those sewing bees and sandwiches—cutting the crusts off! … Who knew?

And a special welcome to our local councillors, who allow us to use the hall and give us some modest funding … and who, umm … who are here to … well, enjoy themselves. We hope.

Little bit of housekeeping. We will go through without an interval. You may hear a little music from the club next door, as it's Jenny Caccielli's twenty-first, but we should be finished well before that kicks off.

Phones off please and if you have any food or lollies now would be a good time to unwrap it.

Now. We, as a company, unfortunately have run into a bit of a hurdle tonight. Nothing insurmountable—never fear—the show will go on. So we are, in fact, a few actors down. But we know the piece so well that we're just going to double and triple up on characters and like the band on board the *Titanic*—play on. (Though hopefully we won't end up sinking … and dying.) We are one player short however—so I wondered—Is there an actor in the house? Anyone here who wouldn't mind getting up and helping us out?

After some audience interaction, perhaps getting someone from the audience (an actor if they're in) and trying them out, then dismissing them—he spots our plant.

You, sir, what's your name?

RICHARD: Ah, Richard … but—

SHANE: And what do you do?

RICHARD: I'm a … pharmacist.

SHANE: Well we need someone to play a doctor so that's close enough. Come on down.

After some support from the audience the plant joins SHANE *onstage.*

RICHARD: I really can't do this, it's not appropriate—

SHANE: We're all nervous, of course you can. So any acting experience Richard?

RICHARD: Well I did play Lady Macb—

SHANE: Uh-uh-uh, don't say it. It's bad luck to say the Scottish play. We just say Lady M.

RICHARD: Oh, okay. I played Lady Emma in high school.

SHANE: All boys school was it?

RICHARD: No.

SHANE: Well, good for you.

RICHARD: Look, I really can't do this.

SHANE: Nonsense, you'll be fine. Tell you what … Barney'll give you a quick crash-course in acting—free of charge. [*Calling off*] Barney!! … Normally he charges three hundred and fifty dollars for a six-week course—but he can summarise …

BARNEY *enters. Gives himself a little clap as he enters.*

Barney Simpson everyone … Barn. Acting in ten seconds.

BARNEY: Articulate. Pause. Sigh, a lot. Eyebrows up for comedy, down for drama. If you need to cry—just say the word for Polish Sausage … 'Cyeva-pe-ci-ci'. And when in doubt—shout. Easy.

RICHARD: For you—

BARNEY: For me, yes, So you're playing the Doctor and the Solicitor. And you WILL need different voices. If the audience get confused, it'll simply ruin the play.

SHANE: Now if you'd just like to make your way backstage, our cast will give you a costume and script …

BARNEY *leads him backstage.*

Big hand for Derek.

RICHARD: [*off*] Richard!

SHANE: Well. Thanks once again for supporting the Middling Cove Players—the North Shore's Premier Am-Dram Society (New members always welcome) … so sit back, or forward, you decide, put your detective hats on and please enjoy opening night of … *Midnight Murder at Hamlington Hall*!!

While some music plays, the stage manager (Karen's NIECE*) reads out a list of who is playing who tonight.*

NIECE: [*voiceover*] Tonight, the parts of Farmer Giles, Colonel Munster and Taffy Hemingway will be played by Barney Simpson. The parts of Gloria, Lady Smythe and Ingrid will be played by Phillipa Chidley. The parts of Margaret and Madame Esmerelda will be played by Aunty Karen. Detective Black will be played by Shane Tweed. The Solicitor will be played by Richard … the chemist. The Doctor will be played by … just about everyone. Benson the butler will be played by whoever's wearing the coat. And the Maid will be played be no-one … [*To herself, thinking the mic is off*] Jeez if they get through this it'll be a fucking miracle.

Yes? … Hi Aunty Karen … No the mic's off … Oh, shit, which button? … Found it …

SHANE: [*voiceover from backstage*] A remote house in Norwich. 1951. Overcast. A chill in the air. A seventy-five per cent chance of rain. Humidity eighty-two per cent, but with a light breeze blowing from the north-east. Perhaps some fog.

SCENE ONE

A study/drawing room. A butler is preparing for guests. Looks out the pretend window.

The butler jacket is way too big for BARNEY. *It's an enormous, heavy tailcoat.*

There is a burst of hip hop, then ... some corny rural period music.

The phone rings. BENSON *answers.*

BENSON: Hamlington Hall.

The phone continues to ring, several times.

Yes, sir, left over the rickety bridge, through the gloomy florist, forest, third driveway after the scarecrow. But don't veer off the road, sir, the terrible Norwich mud is legendary. Once it gets hold of you, you're a goner. Pleasant drive, sir.

The phone rings again. He quickly puts it down. It rings again. He takes it off the hook.

[*To himself*] These clouds look ghastly. Looks like we're in for a fair old belter. We may be cut off by the causeway.

GLORIA *enters. Whatever is* PHILLIPA*'s idea of a diva actress of the era. Perhaps performative and overly dramatic.*

GLORIA: You're not wrong there.

BENSON: Excuse me, ma'am, didn't hear you arrive.

GLORIA: Taxi just dropped me from the station. You're right, those clouds look ominous. You must be Benson.

BENSON: Correct, madam, and you must be …

He consults a list.

Mrs Gloria Whittington. The actress.

GLORIA: [*strikes an actor-y pose*] Ta-dah!

BENSON: Please do make yourself comfortable.

GLORIA: No-one else here?

BENSON: You're the first to arrive, ma'am. I dare say the remainder of the guests will arrive imminently.

BENSON *exits.* BARNEY *leaves the suitcases near the door.*

GLORIA: I do hope so. One does not like to drink on one's own.

BARNEY *returns, trips over the suitcase and pours her the drink.*

She tries and fails to light three cigarettes in a long cigarette holder. She swears under her breath.

PHILLIPA *hums a little 'Don't Rain On My Parade'.*

She spies the guest list. Which is upside down.

Twelve of us eh? No names I recognise … oh, except Detective Black, always a regular at old Hamlington's games nights.

BLACK: [*off*] Thank you, Benson. Mine's the tartan valise.

DOCTOR: [*off*] Watch out for my instruments, they're in the black medical bag.

BLACK: [*off*] Louder.

RICHARD *repeats his line louder.*

BENSON *enters with more bags and leaves the bags in the entry. Then exits.*

DETECTIVE BLACK *and* DOCTOR ERMINGTON *enter.*

DOCTOR ERMINGTON *has a name tag.*

Our plant, RICHARD, *plays the* DOCTOR. *He reads from a script and sometimes needs prompting and blocking direction from* SHANE. *He is nervous at first—but slowly warms into it*

GLORIA: Speak of the devil.

BLACK: He'll be careful. Good man, Benson.

DOCTOR: Right.

BLACK: Do you always travel with your medical bag, Doctor Ermington? Rather odd if you ask me.

At the door KAREN *sneakily gives the* DOCTOR *his medical bag which* RICHARD *has forgotten.*

DOCTOR: Habit, I suppose. You never know when duty may call. Though being a policeman you'd understand that.

BLACK: Detective actually.

GLORIA: Then I assume you brought your handcuffs?

BLACK: Naturally, madam.

GLORIA: Gloria, please.

BLACK: Detective Ernest Black … this is Doctor Freddie Ermington. We shared a cab from the station.

DOCTOR: How do you do?

GLORIA: Well I'll feel better once the mystery of this random invitation is explained. Don't suppose you upstanding gentlemen can shed any light on the matter.

DOCTOR: I'm as in the dark as you I'm afraid.

BLACK: Only what the invitation stated … 'Midday at Hamlington Hall for the eventual reading of Parson Hamlington's last will and testament.'

DOCTOR: 'Eventual' … that's a curious word to employ.

GLORIA: You knew the parson well I believe?

BLACK: And how would you know that, my good lady? Have we met?

GLORIA: No, sir, but I have seen you at one or two of the parson's famous murder-mystery weekends he was so fond of.

RICHARD *is mouthing along with the lines as he follows the script.*

BLACK: Ah-ha.

GLORIA: I'm an actress you see. The parson's favourite. He hired me to play various characters in his little parlour games.

BLACK: Yes I do recognise you now. You played the Psychopathic Russian Heiress at his most recent event, yes?

GLORIA: [*mispronouncing as 'toosh'*] Touché, Detective.

BLACK: Ay.

GLORIA: Eh?

BLACK: Toosh-ay.

GLORIA: Quite.

BLACK: Faces. Never forget them. Part of the job.

There is a very loud screeching-car sound effect.

DOCTOR: My giddy aunt!

BLACK: [*correcting* RICHARD] You're referring to the car.

DOCTOR: Oh sorry.

BENSON *pops his head in.*

BENSON / DOCTOR: I'll just see who that is.

BENSON: I'LL just see who that is.

BLACK: Right you are, Benson. Tell them it's the Norwich countryside, not Monte Carlo!

DOCTOR: Rather intriguing is it not? Wondering just who the other guests may be.

GLORIA: Does one call those at the reading of a will—fellow guests?

Pause—for a moment no-one enters.

Then playboy TAFFY HEMINGWAY, *followed by a nurse,* MARGARET, *enter.*

BARNEY *has false teeth and a toupée as* TAFFY, *which become more difficult to manoeuvre as he swaps from* BENSON *to* TAFFY.

They all leave more bags in the doorway, which people keep tripping over every time they enter and exit.

TAFFY: Good morning, old bricks …

He checks his watch—he isn't wearing one.

No, two minutes after midday—roughly … Good afternoon, all. Taffy Hemingway is the name. Ah perfect … drinks.

He helps himself. BARNEY *tops his glass up with his own flask. He is very hard on the props.*

BLACK: Good afternoon, sir … And this is … your wife?

TAFFY: My wife!! Good God no. This is Margaret something or other. Found her walking here from the station, don't know what she was thinking, it's about to bucket down. Offered her a lift in the 'Beast' … that's the British Racing Green Triumph out front. Hell of an automobile. I'd race her if I could be bothered … the car that is, not Margaret, no offence. Cheers.

MARGARET: Margaret Mathewson. Pleased to meet you all. I take it you all received the invitation to the reading of Parson Hamlington's will?

TAFFY: Why else would we be gathered here like a party of stray woman.

He stops—reinterprets the line.

Sorry, party of strays—comma—woman?

DOCTOR: Thought you might have been a tad more circumspect with a lady on board.

MARGARET: Really it's—

DOCTOR: Bitify old chap.

SHANE: [*correcting him*] Bit iffy.

RICHARD: What?

BLACK: It is a bit … iffy.

TAFFY: Well this is a damn fine welcome. Tried to do the decent thing by helping a fellow traveller get out of the rain, and all I get is brickbats.

SHANE *tries to subtly give* BARNEY *a hint that his* 'TAFFY' *may be a bit too loud.* BARNEY *doesn't get it.*

MARGARET: It's fine really—

TAFFY: Did I at any point put you in danger, miss?

MARGARET: Well overtaking the—

TAFFY: See, nothing at all to cry into your handkerchiefs about, fellows. Wonder if there's any grub to be had, I'm famished … I say, Benson!

BARNEY *realises he needs to be* BENSON.

At the doorway BARNEY *quickly becomes* BENSON, *and pops his head in.*

BENSON: Yes, sir.

TAFFY: Could you get Maid to whip up some snacks. Been a hell of a drive up from London.

BENSON: Of course, sir, I'll call the maid.

BENSON *rings a bell. It makes no sound.*

Ding a ling ling.

They all look offstage. SHANE *makes it clear to the audience who they're all looking at.*

BLACK: Ah the MAID.

BENSON: Some crudités perhaps for the guests please Charlotte while they wait for the rest of the party to assemble.

KAREN *eventually does the voice of the* MAID *under her breath.*

MAID: Certainly, Mr Benson.

RICHARD *looks confused as to where the voice came from.*

BENSON: We're expecting two more taxis from the station any moment. Feel free to wait here. Or by the fire in the library.

MARGARET: I'll wait in my room thank you, Benson.

DOCTOR: I'll take a turn around the library I believe—care to join me, Miss Whittington?

GLORIA: I'd be delighted, Doctor.

MARGARET, GLORIA *and* DOCTOR *leave.*

RICHARD *goes to leave by the wrong door.*

MARGARET: I prefer this door, Doctor.

TAFFY: So … what line are you in, old cock?

BLACK: A bit of this and a bit of that. Mostly that.

TAFFY: Ah, a chap after my own heart. Ducker and a diver. Up top like a swan—down below, feet paddling like a madman. Which is altogether why I'm here compadre. Hoping for a little something in the will eh what.

BLACK: Old Parson Hamlington was a curious fellow that's for certain. And he did love his games.

TAFFY: What is all this about games? Don't tell me the old man was some sort of senile kook. According to my lawyer I'm related to the man.

BLACK: A relation eh? Well that makes things interesting.

TAFFY: You're not wrong there, old cheese.

The sound of a car horn beeping.

Ah, more guests. Perhaps I should …

BARNEY *runs to join the new party entering.*

BENSON: [*off*] Please make yourselves at home here in the drawing room.

LADY SMYTHE *and* MADAME ESMERELDA *enter.*

Stumble over the suitcases.

As new characters enter, SHANE *acknowledges that it's working so far.*

The new characters bring more suitcases on.

PHILLIPA*'s* LADY SMYTHE *is in the vein of Maggie Smith, Margaret Rutherford, Lady Bracknell. Her idea of an aged, upper-class society matron.*

LADY SMYTHE: Thank you, Benson.

There are general introductions. They all get confused as to who is who. A 'who's on first?' type routine. SHANE *guides them through it.*

There is some handshaking business.

BLACK: Lady Smythe, this is Madame Esmerelda.

ESMERELDA: Hello.

LADY SMYTHE: Hello.

BLACK: And I am Detective Black.

The COLONEL *enters with another suitcase.*

Ah Colonel Munster, this is Lady Smythe and Madame Esmerelda.

ESMERELDA: Hello.

LADY SMYTHE: Hello.

COLONEL: Hello. Hello. And you are?

BLACK: Detective Black! … And this is Taffy Hemingway.

COLONEL: Excuse me.

He ducks out to become TAFFY.

BLACK: Well, don't be long …

LADY SMYTHE: Pleasure, Detective Black. Madame Esmerelda.

ESMERELDA: Lady Smythe. Detective.

BARNEY *re-enters as* TAFFY.

TAFFY: Taffy Hemingway, how do you do?

BLACK: Taffy, this is Lady Smythe, Madame Esmerelda.

They shake hands.

ESMERELDA: Taffy.

LADY SMYTHE: Taffy.

TAFFY: And you are?

BLACK / SMYTHE / ESMERELDA: Detective Black!!

TAFFY: Got it.

BLACK: Take a seat, Lady Smythe.

She sits—very slowly.

LADY SMYTHE: That's better. We're lucky to have made it before the rain. No doubt the causeway will overflow as usual.

BLACK: You've been inconvenienced by it before, Lady Smythe?

LADY SMYTHE: I own the estate next door.

BLACK: So you knew him well?

LADY SMYTHE: As well as one can know their eccentric neighbour who was not only the local parson but an avid astronomer, amateur novelist and host of the most marvellous murder-mystery festivals this side of Pemberton-on-Stoke.

TAFFY: That's quite the description.

KAREN, *as* ESMERELDA, *does a wonderful Eastern European accent, and proves to be a very good actor.*

ESMERELDA: He was quite the man. I too dined with Charles—as I knew him—on a regular basis. Our robust discussions on the subjects of religion and the paranormal were my greatest delight.

TAFFY: Paranormal you say?

ESMERELDA: I'm a spiritualist, and a follower of the Wicca faith you see.

BLACK: Wicca? You mean witchcraft?

ESMERELDA: No, sir, I mean Wicca. It's a very misunderstood—

TAFFY: Wicca, witchcraft, it's all baloney and not really relevant to why we're here.

LADY SMYTHE: Prrrrrrrrecisely.

BLACK: May I ask what your connection to Hamlington was, Colonel?

TAFFY: Excuse me, did I see him behind the …

BARNEY *sneaks behind the bookcase and changes into the* COLONEL. TAFFY *and the* COLONEL *talk while* BARNEY *changes.*

COLONEL: Thank you … Hamlington and I served in the war together. He was Charlie Chaplain in my squadron—what? No hang on he was called Charlie and he was a chaplain, that's it. I saved his bacon after he was shot down over Marseille in '41. He was a good man.

KAREN *has thought ahead and gone just offstage to do the* MAID.

MAID: [*off*] It's me … the maid. I've laid out some food in the dining room.

Everyone looks in different directions.

COLONEL: Ah spiffing, worked up quite a hunger listening to you lot.

BLACK: [*pointedly*] Why don't we ALL make way for the new guests so they don't feel overwhelmed.

LADY SMYTHE: Excellent idea.

They all start to leave.

COLONEL: I could do with a little something.
TAFFY: The war eh? Must have been damned exciting, old toast …

They leave.

The SOLICITOR *(played by* RICHARD*) enters, obviously pushed on from the wings, talking to no-one.*

SOLICITOR: No I'm in the dark as much as anyone about the will … despite the fact I'm the man's solicitor. I'll be getting my instructions the same time as you lot—who I take it are the beneficiaries. Are you two family?

GILES *and* INGRID *(*BARNEY *and* PHILLIPA*) hurriedly enter having hastily changed.*

GILES *has a limp.*

He wears big pants with braces over his other costume, and a flat cap.

His limp also causes him to kick every item of furniture and perhaps some audience members as he walks.

GILES: No, sir, I run the Hamlington farm here. Me and the missus. Been 'ere all my life.
SOLICITOR: Uh-huh.

PHILLIPA *is now more confident, acting in her rehearsed role.*

She struggles to nail down her cockney accent—it veers over to Irish mostly.

Perhaps she has plaits.

INGRID: I've never met the man. I work on a Dutch trader that plies its trade between Northern Africa and the Scandinavian territories.
SOLICITOR: How exotic. And you've never had any contact with Parson Hamlington—last remaining heir to the Hamlington fortune?
INGRID: No, sir.

INGRID *exits and runs the long way round backstage.*

SOLICITOR: What the deuce is he up to? Inviting a ragtag bunch of strangers to attend the reading of his will.

BENSON *enters.* SHANE *has put on the oversized butler jacket and stepped in to play* BENSON. *Does his best to copy* BARNEY*'s version. He rings the broken bell.*

BENSON: Ting a ling, ting a ling.
GILES: I guess we're about to find out.

GILES *exits and runs the long way around.*

BENSON: Ladies and gentlemen, please make your way to the drawing room. The reading of the will will now take place—as per the instructions of Parson Charles Hamlington the Third.

TAFFY *and* GLORIA *enter, out of breath.*

TAFFY: Well this is cozy eh what.

TAFFY *exits.*

GLORIA: Don't think I've seen a crowd like this since the parson's last big do.

GLORIA *exits.*

SOLICITOR: Never mind all that. Can we crack on please, everyone?
BENSON: [*buying some time*] We'll just wait for all the other guests shall we?

LADY SMYTHE *enters, out of breath.*

Ah, Lady Smythe …
LADY SMYTHE: Yes— The harder this rain is, the more likely we'll be totally isolated.

Sound effect of rain starts, really loudly.

GILES *enters, out of breath. He has to shout over the rain sound.*

GILES: She's coming down now!
BENSON: Perhaps it's not quite as heavy as we thought!!

The rain sound effect lowers.

ESMERELDA: May I remind you that a man has died! Can we show some respect for the departed?
BENSON: Ladies and gentlemen, thank you for attending the reading of the last will and testament of Parson Hamlington. I have been instructed to play this short cinescope film.

BENSON *pulls down the screen and plays a (prop) reel to reel projector.*

The film is supposed to be Parson Hamlington ... obviously one of the actors backstage (à la Dorian Gray).

A live-feed to backstage comes up on the screen—but no-one appears on camera.

SHANE *realises, as do the others, that he has no-one to cover for this part. His first big blunder.*

KAREN*'s* NIECE *runs down, grabs a wig and costume and appears on the screen.*

While she does, BARNEY *and* LADY SMYTHE *improvise.*

GILES / LADY SMYTHE: These old projectors take a while to warm up … valves and … download to the mainframe … [*etc.*]

The NIECE *finally appears on the screen (we either use our real SM or it's pre-recorded).*

HAMLINGTON (NIECE): [*reading*] Good afternoon. I am Charles Hamlington. Those who know me, know my love of a good murder mystery, laughs heartily. Before I die … This is my chance to play one last game. Hidden around the manor are clues and riddles for you to find and solve. You have until midnight tonight to prove you deserve a share in the Hamlington estate. You may leave now … However—if you choose to play and don't solve your conundrum by midnight … you will die. Hahahahahhaha! Let the game begin!

There is a general brouhaha of 'This is mad!', 'I've never!', 'He's insane!', etc. ...

BARNEY: Rhubarb! Rhubarb!

RICHARD *reads the stage direction.*

The NIECE *exits and the backstage camera switches off.*

LADY SMYTHE: This is preposterous.

ESMERELDA: I think it's quite thrilling myself.

SOLICITOR: I agree, but as his solicitor—

GILES: Solicitor?? And you didn't know about this ridiculous charade?

SOLICITOR: I assure you I did not. Did you know, Colonel?

BARNEY *sighs. He can't go off and change again.*

GILES: The colonel said to say … 'Classic Hamlington I must say.'

ESMERELDA: I quite agree, this is SO Charlie to mock death like this. What do you think, Taffy?

GILES: Taffy told me … he has no strong feelings on the matter.

BENSON: Time is of the essence, ladies and gentlemen. Is there anyone who wishes to leave now?

All look at each other for a long, dramatic moment.

Very well. We shall meet again at midnight.

There is a pause.

Sorry, were you going to say something, Doctor?

SHANE *gives him the medical bag—then exits quickly to remove the* BENSON *coat.*

DOCTOR: Of course … sorry … Hold on just a moment. We don't think anyone will actually die? It's just a game?

GILES: You sound awfully like the solicitor, Doctor. That could be confusing.

DOCTOR: [*doing* GILES*' voice*] It's just a game.

GILES: Not that one.

DOCTOR: [*trying another voice*] It's just a game.

GILES: Better.

DOCTOR: [*finding his cockney* DOCTOR *voice*] It's just a game.

GILES: Brilliant … Well I for one am bang up for the game.

BLACK: [*entering*] I'm with Colonel Munster.

GILES: No!

BLACK: If I can't find and solve a couple of clues, what sort of dick am I? Good luck to us all.

Blackout.

Some scene-change music.

SCENE TWO

Lights up. On stage are GLORIA, *the* DOCTOR *(now* BARNEY, *with a name tag) and the* SOLICITOR.

BARNEY *makes a show of showing off the bag and name tag.*

DOCTOR: Yes, now I am a doctor alright.
SOLICITOR: So … Doctor.

He accidentally throws his script. It goes everywhere.

GLORIA: So not even his solicitor knew of his insane plan eh?
SOLICITOR: [*panicking*] Er … no. I … no.

GLORIA *and the* DOCTOR *help him out.*

GLORIA: You're probably thinking … why am I not searching?? I believe I've already found my clue. En pleine vue, as the French would say. Doctor, would you be kind enough to take down that portrait of the parson?
DOCTOR: Of course. As the doctor I shall.

He does so. As he does BARNEY *accidentally puts his hand through the face of the portrait.*

SOLICITOR: Oh shit … I mean oh dear.
GLORIA: You see, in that portrait the good parson is sporting a pocket kerchief of a particular shade of purple. His favourite production of mine was a highly lauded show at the Almeida called—*Miss Fanny's Lilac Hanky*.
DOCTOR: Damn it you're right. Here on the back! An envelope with your name on it!
GLORIA: The game is quite simple see.
SOLICITOR: It's umm …

He tries to be part of the scene—but with no script, is lost.

PHILLIPA *saves him again.*

GLORIA: I guess you're thinking 'You still have to solve the riddle though', eh? I would respond with 'Yes, but isn't this fizzing good fun!'
DOCTOR: I must admit, I am rather warming to the whole idea.

RICHARD *still struggling.*

SOLICITOR: Should I …

Now BARNEY *saves him.*

DOCTOR: And I'll bet you're wondering what the consequences of not succeeding by midnight are?? Well I would've said—'Come now, old chap.'

GLORIA: And you may say … 'You don't seriously believe that anyone will actually be harmed in any way.'

SOLICITOR: And I would've said—

GLORIA: You would have said something along the lines of … 'It's a game. You'll just die in the game I suppose.'

DOCTOR: And perhaps have added … 'It's metaphorical'.

SOLICITOR: It's metapho—

DOCTOR: No need to repeat it.

GLORIA: And of course you won't receive your share of the estate—if that can be believed.

BENSON *arrives with a package for the* SOLICITOR. *He opens it, it's a new script.*

SOLICITOR: Got it!! … Oh believe it.

GLORIA *reads her riddle.*

GLORIA: Hmmm … a tricky rhyming riddle to be sure … ouch!

DOCTOR: Are you alright?

GLORIA: Oh yes, just a paper cut.

SOLICITOR: Any luck in solving it? You seem to have quite the knack …

GLORIA: Well I have played many of the parson's murderous games before … Ah-ha!

DOCTOR: By George I think she's got it.

SOLICITOR: Am I George?

GLORIA: I don't want to sound overconfident boys … but I do believe—

There is the sound of a crack of lightning.

All the lights go out. Dramatic music sting.

DOCTOR: I—

The music sting continues.

—say.

The SOLICITOR *puts his phone torch on.*

SOLICITOR: Well this is most unusual.

DOCTOR: Probably the storm.

SOLICITOR: [*trying to read in the dark*] These old horses … ancient wiring no doubt.

The lights come back on.

DOCTOR: There we go.

GLORIA *is lying on the chaise.*

Miss Whittington, are you alright? You were about to reveal your clue.

SOLICITOR: What the devil is she doing?

The DOCTOR *goes to her.*

DOCTOR: Miss Whittington?? Miss Whittington!

SOLICITOR: What's wrong?

DOCTOR: She's … she's dead.

SOLICITOR: She can't be.

He goes to her.

DOCTOR: She is.

SOLICITOR: Good God. Help I say!! Benson!!

BENSON *(hastily played by* KAREN, *now in the oversized tailcoat) and* BLACK *enter.*

BLACK: What is it? What's all the screaming?

BENSON: Is the lady alright?

SOLICITOR: Call for an ambulance!

BENSON: I'm afraid it won't make it over the causeway now, sir.

BLACK: You mean there is no way in or out of here until this storm passes?

BENSON: That's exactly what I mean.

DOCTOR: It's pointless anyway. She's dead. Poisoned I'd venture.

BLACK: What happened?

DOCTOR: The lights went out for a few seconds … when they came back on …

SOLICITOR: Dead. She had just uncovered her clue.

BLACK: You mean this?

He takes the clue from her hand. She holds on to it too tight. He struggles to get it out of her hand.

[*Reading*] 'The thespian's clue was easy. Make no mistake, the game is real. Time is ticking, people. Midnight comes with zeal!'

SOLICITOR: This can't be happening! Murder! … Most awful … right here before our eyes!!

RICHARD *delivers this line quite well.*

DOCTOR: There you go!

BLACK: Get a hold of yourself, man. Who else was here?

DOCTOR: Just he and I.

SOLICITOR: Surely you don't think we had anything to do with it.

BLACK: What leads you to conclude it was poisoning doctor?

DOCTOR: Well, the speed of the asphyxiation. The frothing around the mouth. And being dead.

SOLICITOR: A blow dart perhaps. Through the window?

DOCTOR: Come come man, we're not in the Congo.

SOLICITOR: Or perhaps a very tiny bullet.

BLACK: Don't be a fool. Anyone can see it's from this paper cut. Doctor, I assume you carry poisonous substances among your medicines.

DOCTOR: Why of course. What sort of doctor would I be if I didn't carry poisonous substances with me?

BLACK: And where are they?

DOCTOR: In my bag—upstairs in my room. Benson deposited it there.

They all look to the medical bag that the DOCTOR *is holding.*

BLACK: Is it though?

DOCTOR: Yes. It is.

BLACK: Very well. Let's agree to disagree. Ah Colonel!

DOCTOR: Excuse me a moment.

Goes behind the bookcase and moves some books aside and speaks through them.

COLONEL: What's all the commotion?

MARGARET *enters.*

MARGARET: Yes, what's going on?

BLACK: Miss Whittington is dead.

MARGARET *screams. Not used to this level of performance,* PHILLIPA, *as* GLORIA, *sits bolt upright.*

All on stage now improvise a way out of the situation. BARNEY *is constantly improvising badly: 'She looks fine.' 'That's a scream. Do you have vocal training?' 'She's definitely definitely dead.'*

PHILLIPA *doesn't know whether to lie down or join in. It's an impro debacle.*

SHANE *eventually breaks it up saying loudly—*

BLACK: LET'S ALL JUST MOVE ON THEN SHALL WE!!

He cues the bio box to go to blackout.

It does except for one random light.

He cues the music, but a Spotify ad comes blaring on: 'Sign up for Spotify Premium now and get uninterrupted music 24/7—'

Eventually the scene-change music plays and SHANE *is satisfied.*

He changes the time on the grandfather clock as he exits.

SCENE THREE

GILES, MARGARET *and* LADY SMYTHE *are searching the room.*

Throughout the scene BARNEY *(as* GILES*) is adjusting—and getting tangled in—his braces, which he has put on wrong. They all help and get caught up.*

LADY SMYTHE: How on earth did I get caught up in all this, Giles?

GILES: [*re the braces*] And how did I get caught up in ... P'raps he knew of your money troubles, Lady Smythe.

LADY SMYTHE: I beg your pardon?

GILES: P'raps this is his way of 'elpin' oot.

MARGARET: Assuming you survive the night.

LADY SMYTHE: That's rather dramatic, young lady.

MARGARET: A woman was murdered in this very room. I hardly think a little skepticism is dramatic.

GILES: [*to* MARGARET] I know you don't I?

MARGARET: How can I be expected to answer that?

GILES: You were the parson's nose.

MARGARET: Nurse.

GILES: You looked after him when he was ailing these past few months.

MARGARET: Correct. He was one of my patients.
LADY SMYTHE: Seems he must have been quite unhinged to invent this deadly game of his.
MARGARET: The parson was a … unique gentleman. He talked of his love of mysteries over and over.
GILES: So why include you in his list of inheritors?
LADY SMYTHE: Or victims.

PHILLIPA *makes unnecessary interjections whenever* KAREN*'s acting is going well.*

MARGARET: I was a good listener. At least I thought I was. Perhaps he secretly hated me and this is his form of punishment. He resented me caring for him as he lay dying and this is his revenge!! Oh God, I'm going to die tonight!
LADY SMYTHE: There she goes being dramatic again.

PHILLIPA *looks to* BARNEY *for support.*

MARGARET: I'm going to die! We're all going to die!!
GILES: Now now, girly, calm yourself.

GILES *slaps her. A bad theatre slap.* KAREN *dodges and blocks his slap.*

BARNEY *keeps trying.*

KAREN: What the fuck?

KAREN *expertly grabs his arm and twists it behind his back, then pins him on to the sofa.*

BARNEY *thinks she might be pulling a knife.*

BARNEY: Don't shiv me!
LADY SMYTHE: Nurse Margaret, control yourself …

KAREN *lets* BARNEY *up.*

Now what was your main connection to Hamlington?
MARGARET: My main task was administering his medicines.
LADY SMYTHE: Have you checked the medicine cabinet?
MARGARET: I shall look immediately … apologies for my undignified outburst.
GILES: We're all on edge tonight.

MARGARET *leaves.*

BARNEY *and* PHILLIPA *look at each other, still unsure about* KAREN.

Jesus Christ.

LADY SMYTHE: Well handled, Giles.

GILES: She was quite overwrought … and quite scary.

LADY SMYTHE: [*commenting on* KAREN*'s acting*] A bit too 'overwrought' I think … Join me in a drink … Giles.

GILES: Thank you, ma'am. Just the one.

LADY SMYTHE *pours him a drink.*

But then the drinking fountain sprays in the wrong direction, misses her glass and makes a mess on GILES*'s pants. He moves his glass but she misses again.*

Perhaps she swears. She blames others and the props for any mistakes.

More water sprays on the floor.

The actors continue to slip on this spill for the rest of the show.

LADY SMYTHE: Oh bother. Well, perhaps this is a sign I shouldn't tarry. To the conservatory!

She leaves. GILES *sips his drink. There is only the tiniest amount in it.* BARNEY *takes a sip of his own hip flask. He pulls up a chair and sits with his back to the audience.*

GILES: Think, Giles. Where's this bloody clue hid?

BARNEY *slides out of the chair and surreptitiously gets out of* GILES*'s pants and sneaks off.*

After a moment TAFFY *strolls in casually—and* INGRID *enters from opposite door.*

Throughout the scene BARNEY *makes a body out of cushions and puts* GILES*'s hat on it so it looks like* GILES *is sitting in the chair.*

INGRID: Taffy.

BARNEY *has forgotten the voice, he does* GILES*'s voice.*

TAFFY: Ingrid. Any luck? [*Trying again*] Any luck?

INGRID: Nothing yet … your voice, Taffy … it's—
TAFFY: Just a … cold—
INGRID: Were you close? Thank you for the drink.

BARNEY *hasn't given her the drink.*

TAFFY: You're welcome … Close? I never met the old fool. Don't go in for family much … or religion. Fast cars, women and horse racing are my game. And not in that order … [*Re the voice*] there it is.
INGRID: So do you intend on even looking for your clue?
TAFFY: No … Once that causeway opens up I'm back to London and straight to my lawyers.

And I've got my old friends Smith & Wesson here if anybody tries any funny business.

He pats his pocket. He's forgotten his gun. Gets out a finger gun.

INGRID: That looks heavy, can I hold it?

He gives her the finger gun. She makes the finger gun. Weighs it in her hand.

TAFFY: Careful, I'd better take that back.

He makes the finger gun. Now they are both holding a gun. Eventually he pockets the finger gun.

I say, who's that in the chair?
INGRID: It's that farmer fellow. Must be napping. Perhaps he's already solved his.

INGRID *leaves.*

TAFFY: Good luck to him … Well she's gone. Rude.

TAFFY *goes to pour himself a drink.* BARNEY *slips on the spill that* PHILLIPA *made. Has to drink out of the bottle.*

Might as well join you in a nip, old bean.

After a few sips, he coughs a bit.

What the devil … not going down quite right …

He starts to choke.

I say, old banana … I may need a little … help.

He goes over to GILES *(the cushion man).*

GILES: 'Elp me … I'm dying too.

TAFFY: Good God!! I say … Help! … Bit of help here!!

TAFFY, *choking on the drink, stumbles around the room. He hits his head on the fireplace. Offstage we hear* BLACK *and the* DOCTOR *arrive.*

BLACK: What is it? What the devil?

DOCTOR: [*now in his* DOCTOR *voice*] He's choking. Spit it out, man!

BLACK: It's the drink. Look, the glass or bottle is still in his hand. Good heavens … He's dead … Taffy.

TAFFY *is now lying dead on the couch.*

And another one!! Giles? … Yes Giles! —Dead as a doorknob.

DOCTOR: Both with drinks in their hands.

BLACK: And … [*Sniffing*] brandy on their breaths.

DOCTOR: Do you think it was … ?

BLACK: The brandy. Yes.

DOCTOR: Poisoned. Again.

BLACK: I see a pattern here, Doctor.

DOCTOR: [*sniffing glass*] There's a chemical in there for certain.

BLACK *rubs a bit of the substance on his teeth.*

BLACK: Arsenic. What the ghost of Mary Shelley is Hamlington up to?

DOCTOR: This is most troubling, Detective. He's not even waiting till midnight.

BLACK: My suspicion is, this is another's hand altogether.

BENSON *enters (played by* KAREN*).*

BENSON: There appears to be a body on the couch … [*Seeing* GILES] and another … someone's been busy.

BLACK: Here, Benson, pour this lot down the drain. And throw something over these stiffs—don't want to scare the ladies.

BENSON: Ladies are not that easily scared, sir.

BENSON *leaves.*

DOCTOR: You don't think it could be Benson, do you?

BLACK: Well he certainly had access to the alcohol.

DOCTOR: But the butler? Seems such a cliché.

BLACK: If there's one thing I've learned in my years at Scotland Yard—it's to never discount the bleeding obvious.

Blackout.

Music. SHANE *moves the hands of the clock forward again.*

SCENE FOUR

MADAME ESMERELDA *and* COLONEL MUNSTER *enter carrying envelopes. The* COLONEL *has a head bandage.*

ESMERELDA: Ah Colonel Mustard, are you okay? … I see you too have managed to find your rhyming riddle.

COLONEL: Finally dawned on me. Hamlington and I served together … 'served'. It was in the dumb waiter.

ESMERELDA: Well, our greatest disagreements were of the ecclesiastic kind. So mine was in the chapel. Shall we?

The COLONEL *opens his envelope, but it's empty.* ESMERELDA *opens hers and it's empty too.*

KAREN *has forgotten to set them. She mouths 'sorry'.*

COLONEL: [*struggling to improvise*] 'When Apollo, wearing a cardigan, ate his peas … the whole of the world was infested with fleas.' … Hmmmm.

ESMERELDA *pretends to read hers.*

ESMERELDA: 'If a yellow horse's mane scrubs up well—ride that beast to the depths of hell.' Hmmm.

They pause, waiting for SHANE *to enter.*

KAREN *repeats her line.*

'If a yellow horse's mane scrubs up well, ride that beast to the depths of hell!'

She tries again.

'HORSE'S MANE SCRUBS UP WELL RIDE IT TO THE DEPTHS OF HELL!!' That was the CLUE!!

SHANE *eventually realises and enters.*

BLACK: Ahh congratulations, I see you've uncovered half of your conundrum.

He offers to take the riddles.

Now allow me—I don't mean to lose another victim.

ESMERELDA: What do you mean 'another' victim?

BLACK: Haven't you heard? Two more murders. Some guff in the brandy. That lead-footed cove Taffy Hemingway and poor old Giles.

COLONEL: [*faltering and drinking from flask*] ... So the playboy and the farmer?

BLACK: That's what I just said ... seems there's someone among us who's decided to change the game to suit their own devious devices.

Pause.

Then you say ...

BARNEY *is starting to falter. Forgetting lines, etc.*

COLONEL: You mean ... do you? ... It ... is ... someone who ...

BLACK: That's right, Colonel Mustard. Someone who wishes to knock off any competitors and take the whole blessed lot for him ... or herself.

COLONEL: Then check your crystal ... cards ... 'madame', and tell us who's knocking us out ... off.

ESMERELDA: I fully intend to put my skills as a psychic detective to the—

BLACK: Psychic detective! ... Come now ...

ESMERELDA: You may laugh, sir—but I ask you this. Have you ever heard of the Strange Disappearance of the Whitney Twelve?

BLACK: Of course.

ESMERELDA: The Curious Case of the Horton-on-Wye Gumboot Killer?

BLACK: Yes.

ESMERELDA: The Unexplained Sightings on the SS *Belvedere*?

BLACK: Yes, madame.

ESMERELDA: These are all police matters of which your lot had no answers—and turned to me for help.

BLACK: Hmmm, impressive.

ESMERELDA: Thank you.

BLACK: Not at all.

ESMERELDA: Then I look forward.

BLACK: To what exactly?

ESMERELDA: Exactly.

BLACK: Precisely.

ESMERELDA: Elementary.

They get caught in a dialogue loop and repeat it a few times. Each time more panicky.

BLACK: Thank you.
ESMERELDA: Not at all.
BLACK: Then I look forward.
ESMERELDA: To what exactly?
BLACK: Exactly.
ESMERELDA: Precisely.
BLACK: Elementary.
ESMERELDA: Thank you.
BLACK: Then I look forward.
ESMERELDA: To what exactly?
BLACK: Exactly.
ESMERELDA: Precisely.
BLACK: Elementary.
ESMERELDA: Thank you.
BLACK: Not at all.
ESMERELDA: Exactly.
BLACK: Exactly.
ESMERELDA: Exactly.
BLACK: Exactly … What do you say, Colonel?
COLONEL: Impressive.
ESMERELDA: Thank you.
COLONEL: Not at all.
ESMERELDA: Then I look forward.
COLONEL: To what exactly?
ESMERELDA: Exactly.
COLONEL: Precisely.
ESMERELDA: Elementary.
COLONEL: Impressive.
ESMERELDA: Thank you.
COLONEL: I'm getting woozy, help—

BLACK *snaps them out of it.*

BLACK: ACTUALLY … While we've been talking I've managed to solve your little rhyming riddles. If you please …

They hand over their riddles. They're blank.

SHANE *looks to* BARNEY.

COLONEL: Mine reads … [*Trying to remember what the made up earlier*] 'When Narcissus flew in a balloon to the moon, he came quite close to the unpunctual groom.'

It's close to what he said before. Sort of.

BLACK: Okay … Hmmmm … 'When Narcissus flew to the moon' … Narcissus was Greek and flying to the moon is impossible—therefore we have an impossible Greek. Who is an impossible Greek? … Zorba. 'He came quite close to the unpunctual groom' … Zorba is quite close to zebra—whose black-and-white colouring is similar to that of a groom. When one is unpunctual they are also late—which can also mean dead … ergo—a dead zebra. If you would be so kind as to look in the mouth of the dead zebra mounted on the wall in the smoking room, Colonel … But here … use these.

He hands him some long tweezers. BARNEY *exits and returns a moment later with a red silk handkerchief in the tweezers.*

COLONEL: A red silk kerchief with 'Congratulations' embroidered on it. Well done, man.

ESMERELDA: Very impressive, Detective Black. But why the tweezers?

BLACK: I'll wager these silk trophies are also laced with poison. Our offender would have made sure anyone who got this far would go no further in the contest. [*To* ESMERELDA] And what of your riddle?

ESMERELDA *starts to read it …*

ESMERELDA: Oh for God's sake, it's in the sink.

BLACK: And how did you figure that out?

ESMERELDA: [*exiting*] I'm psychic remember.

SHANE: [*quietly*] Thank you.

She grabs the tweezers, runs out. We hear her having trouble finding her prop. She pops her head back in.

ESMERELDA: Keep talking, gents—I'll be back.

While they are offstage doing this, SHANE *attempts to engage* BARNEY *in some covering banter.* BARNEY *is tapped out now and can't think of anything to say.*

SHANE: She'll be back any moment, Colonel Munster.
BARNEY: It's Mustard! Wait, no … it's Munster. Commodore Munster … I mean Commodore Holden. No, that's the car … 'Colonel' is fine.
SHANE: And do you have any … hobbies, Colonel?
BARNEY: Yes … I … No … Just … the war.
SHANE: How was that?
BARNEY: Loud.

The impro drags on.

BARNEY *offers* SHANE *his hip flask.*

Eventually ESMERELDA *re-enters.*

SHANE: [*to himself*] Thank Christ.
ESMERELDA: Found it!
COLONEL: I'm out.
ESMERELDA: Come, Detective—you and I need to combine our talents and interview the others in person.
BLACK: And you, Colonel?
COLONEL: I … do not know what is happening … I'm starched … thirsty … parched? … Parched … I'm parched …

BARNEY *starts to take off his clothes.* SHANE *and* KAREN *stop him. They hustle him offstage.*

BARNEY *is making strange, panicky noises.*

PHILLIPA *walks out, says 'Hit it' to the stage manager, starts to belt out 'Don't Rain On My Parade'.*

BLACK: Thank you, Ingrid—for cheering us all up.

He motions to go to blackout.

Blackout.

In the blackout we hear BARNEY *apologising in the wings.*

BARNEY: I'm sorry.
KAREN: No-one noticed. Hang in there, Barn. Nearly there.

Some scene-change music plays.

SCENE FIVE

INGRID *and the* DOCTOR *(now* SHANE*) enter from opposite doors.*

SHANE *has the doctor name tag and carries the bag.*

INGRID: Ah, Doctor.

DOCTOR: Forgive me, I don't think I caught your name before—what with all these people getting murdered.

INGRID: It's Ingrid.

DOCTOR: Oh how rude of me, I didn't divulge my name. The tag just says 'Doctor'. Ermington. Freddie Ermington. Fred Pennington-Ermington actually … the Third. Doctor Fredrick Pennington-Ermington the Third. Got there in the end.

INGRID: Pleasure to meet you, Doctor. Did you know the parson at all?

DOCTOR: I didn't even know what the man looked like.

INGRID: I'm assuming that's him in the portrait.

> *They look at the portrait, which has a hole in the face (from the accident in Scene Two).* RICHARD *puts his face through the hole in the portrait to replace the missing one.*
>
> *The* DOCTOR *gasps when he sees it.*

Are you alright, Doctor? You've turned positively grey.

DOCTOR: It can't be … By Jove, I DO know the parson after all. Many years ago, this man married me.

INGRID: How scandalous!

> *The portrait drops off the wall, but* RICHARD *stays in place and strikes the same pose as the portrait.*

DOCTOR: No, I mean I was married by this man. He performed the ceremony for myself and my childhood love—Rebecca. We met during our years of study at Oxford, a university. However tragedy struck on our honeymoon. Our steamer went down off the coast of Algiers. I was one of the lucky ones. She was not.

INGRID: How dreadful … Wait … What year was this?

DOCTOR: The summer of 1935.

INGRID: Strange. The summer of '35 was exactly when I was rescued by a Moroccan trader.

DOCTOR: How odd.

INGRID: They found me washed up on a rocky outcrop. Barely alive, and suffering from amnesia. All I had on me was this garnet ring.

DOCTOR: Oh good heavens!! Look here …

He shows her his ring. He can't find it and has to hide the fact from the audience.

INGRID: [*gasps dramatically*] They're identical.

DOCTOR: These were our betrothal rings … Rebecca! … It can't be … but your pale alabaster skin and auburn hair??

INGRID: Sunkissed after years at sea … and hair bleached blonde by the cruel Mediterranean sun.

DOCTOR: Rebecca. Oh my darling Becky.

INGRID: I have no memory of a husband … But the rings … it's IRRRREFUTABLE …

DOCTOR: Allow me to take you in my arms. Perhaps the closeness of our hearts will reignite our passion.

INGRID: Doctor, I—

DOCTOR: Sssshhh.

He takes her in his arms. Then kisses her.

Was that okay?

INGRID: Yeah … that was … nice.

DOCTOR: You do know I've … loved you for all these years.

INGRID: I know. But you were engaged … I was told on the boat. And I was off and on with Damian … one of … the crew …

DOCTOR: So maybe now, the timing feels right?

INGRID: It kind of does.

They kiss again.

They get back into the scene.

Oh Freddie.

DOCTOR: Oh Rebecca.

INGRID: Oh Freddie … it's all coming back to me.

DOCTOR: But this is quite unbelievable.

We hear the sound of the mic check from the party next door. It continues intermittently throughout the scene.

The SOLICITOR *and* MARGARET *enter.*

MARGARET: Well it's nearly midnight ... TIME IS TICKING DETECTIVE ... and I've yet to find a clue.

SOLICITOR: No luck here either.

SHANE *(as* DOCTOR*) out of nowhere says ...*

DOCTOR: I say ... I'm parched!

As discussed earlier, they all, including BARNEY *from offstage, now wearing his robe, join him at the bookshelf ... they pretend to look at books or find business to cover their conversation.*

SHANE: [*to the assembled actors, in a whisper*] Okay, well done, everyone, but we're running long. The party's about to start next door. We need to get to the final scene quickly. I'll wrap it up ... just the plot points.

RICHARD: There's a plot?

KAREN: We're really going to have to motor.

SHANE: I know ... Guys ... We're going off-script.

They all gasp.

PHILLIPA: Won't that be confusing?

BARNEY: I'm well past that.

SHANE: Just stick with me, team. Follow my lead.

PHILLIPA: It's going well though, don't you think?

BARNEY: I've had better nights.

KAREN: It was actually almost worth getting arrested for this.

RICHARD: Whatever it takes ... bring it on, baby!

SHANE: Once more unto the breach, dear friends!! Let's hustle!!

He claps his hands and they jump back into the scene.

BARNEY *goes off and puts on the* BENSON *tailcoat.*

From here to the end of the play there is a manic energy.

BLACK: Well, here we all are, all of us ... altogether.

ESMERELDA: Not quite all, Detective. Are you forgetting that three of our number have been murdered in cold hard blood?

BLACK: I most certainly have not forgotten.

ESMERELDA: Why don't we start by showing our cards as it were?

INGRID: Meaning?

ESMERELDA: By a show of ... handkerchiefs ... who amongst us managed to solve their riddle.

BLACK: Excellent suggestion, Madame Esmerelda.

COLONEL, ESMERELDA, DOCTOR, INGRID, LADY SMYTHE *and* MARGARET *all lay a silk hanky on the table.*

All except MARGARET *wear gloves.*

That leaves myself and Parson Hamlington's solicitor, whose name is yet to be mentioned for some reason, as the only guests not to have completed the game.

By this point, RICHARD *has got the gist of things, and he is acting his part very well. It feels like he is one of the company.*

SOLICITOR: And the mysterious maid.
BLACK: Forget the maid.
LADY SMYTHE: And Benson here.

BARNEY *enters dressed as* BENSON, *but he's forgotten to put his pants on.*

BENSON: Correction, Lady Smythe—I too found the clue the parson hid.

He pulls a red silk hanky out of his pocket—it is connected to a series of coloured scarves which he continues to pull out and eventually hold near his face.

And here it is!

Everyone gasps.

BLACK: Benson! The kerchief! Put it down!
BENSON: Never! I …

He starts to falter. The poisoned hanky eventually asphyxiates him. BARNEY *does a long and highly theatrical death, extricating himself from the tailcoat and laying it face down on the sofa.*

ALL: Benson!! / Help him!! / Dear God!! / Not another!! / Speed it up, Barney! [*etc.*]
BLACK: Stand back.

BLACK *checks his pulse.*

I can confirm … he's dead … murdered.

Everyone gasps.

SOLICITOR: Well that's one less person you all have to share the loot with.

LADY SMYTHE: How can you be so callous?

SOLICITOR: [*hysterical*] Because I am next in line to be murdered, madam, that is why!!

KAREN *slaps the hysterical* RICHARD.

LADY SMYTHE *finds a note in* BENSON*'s pocket.*

LADY SMYTHE: I say … look here.

She hands it to BLACK.

BLACK: An unopened envelope … [*Reading*] 'To be read aloud at midnight upon completion of the game.'

SOLICITOR: What are you waiting for, Detective?

BLACK *opens it and reads.*

BLACK: 'The good news is … you have all won! The game was just a game— you will ALL receive a share in the Hamlington Estate. With the exception of my solicitor—Edward … '

ALL: Aah … Edward!

BLACK: [*reading*] 'Toodles. Parson Charles Hamlington.'

They ALL *cheer.*

I hate to burst your bubbles, ladies and gentlemen, but there is still the small matter of three—

ESMERELDA: [*indicating* BENSON] Four!

BLACK: Four … deaths to consider. If *Hamlington* didn't mean us to die, then someone in this room is a murderer!!

ALL: Gasp!

BARNEY *gasps and audibly says 'Rhubarb, rhubarb'.*

BLACK: [*very fast*] Jesus, Colonel! … If we go back to the death of Miss Gloria Whittington. She received a small paper cut on her finger. This suggests she or the killer had access to stationery supplies and therefore knew their whereabouts. Upon examination of the body of the arrogant playboy Taffy Hemingway—as well as consuming the tainted brandy, he appeared to have come in contact with a slow-acting stupification agent administered by hypodermic needle. Farmer Giles however, drunk from the poisoned brandy, which was most likely planted by a staff member.

There is more music or speeches from the party next door. Perhaps they are singing 'Happy Birthday' to Jenny.

ESMERELDA: Obviously not Benson. Excuse me …

KAREN runs offstage and runs next door to the club to get them to pipe down.

BLACK: Further investigation showed me that the silk kerchiefs were indeed soaked in cyanide and were deadly to the touch. Which accounts for all of us except our erstwhile nurse.

SOLICITOR: And that damn maid!!

BLACK: FORGET THE DAMN MAID!

We hear from the party next door—KAREN has burst in.

KAREN: [*off*] HEY HEY!

The music stops.

WE ARE NEARLY DONE!! PLEASE SHUT THE FUCK UP. JUST GIVE US FIVE MINUTES!! … And happy birthday, Jenny.

BLACK: [*stretching for time*] Which … leaves … only …

KAREN runs back in, out of breath.

You … Nurse Margaret!

MARGARET: What?!

BLACK: You may look and play the innocent, but who had access to the brandy? Who had access to hypodermics and the expertise to administer them? Who had been employed here at Hamlington Hall? And who was the only one in this very room not to handle their cyanide-soaked silk kerchief with gloves, because she knew that hers was not tainted?

BARNEY is by now slumped, broken in a chair.

COLONEL: Is it me?

BLACK: You, Miss Mathewson.

MARGARET: Alright!! Yes it was me!! When I got wind of this crazy game the parson had in mind, I decided to improve my odds of winning. Knock the rest of you out of contention and take the lot for myself. Me—the one who deserved it. I had to feed and bathe him. Read him countless mysteries and crime potboilers.

BLACK: No doubt these novels are where she got the ideas for her criminal procedures.

INGRID: That Agatha Christie has a lot to answer for.

BLACK: Nurse Mathewson—you're under arrest.

INGRID: Wait! … Can I just say, Detective … before you go on. Congratulations for steering us through this difficult night.

BARNEY *picks up on what* PHILLIPA *is doing.*

COLONEL: Yes, very well done, Detective. Sorry if I let the team down … I did my best.

MARGARET: No, Colonel, you were great. You soldiered on, in the face of real … hardship.

COLONEL: Thanks Margaret …

BLACK: And Margaret, even though you have committed a heinous crime … you played the game exceptionally.

MARGARET: Thank you, Detective. You may not believe it, but this was just what I needed. I think I've found something that I'm actually pretty good at.

BLACK: You are. Very.

INGRID: And apologies if I got a little tense … but, I don't care, because I think I may have found a long-lost love in Doctor Freddie Pennington-Ermington … wherever he is.

COLONEL: Here here.

SHANE *is touched.*

BLACK: Thank you … all. We did it, didn't we. This ragtag bunch of amateur … sleuths, pulled it off … So, as I was saying … Nurse Mathewson … I'm placing you under arrest.

MARGARET *pulls out a gun. Still a finger gun.*

MARGARET: I don't think so!

INGRID: She's got Taffy's gun!

BARNEY *looks at his finger.*

BLACK: Give me the gun, Margaret.

MARGARET: Never!

She fires the gun. They wait for a delayed gunshot sound effect.

INGRID: Detective!

BLACK: It's just a flesh wound.

MARGARET: You'll have to catch me first.

She fires the gun at the lights. They all go out.

SOLICITOR: The lights!

BARNEY: Has she gone rogue?

The sound of the window smashing.

BLACK: She's gone through the window!

All crowd around the window. Lights come back on ... somehow.

INGRID: She's running towards the car.
COLONEL: Car?
BLACK: Taffy's car—keep up.

Sound effects of car starting and driving off.

INGRID: She's driving away.
SOLICITOR: She's headed for that tree.

Sound effects of car skidding and crashing.

BLACK: She's crashed the car.
INGRID: It's gone up in flames.

Perhaps outside the window, KAREN *does a cheap-looking explosion effect. Orange light and birds on sticks flying away.*

COLONEL: Now she's sinking in the mud. The Norwich mud … it's like quicksand remember, from Scene One?
BLACK: Yes alright, she's sinking.
SOLICITOR: She's barely visible.
INGRID: She's trying to say something.
COLONEL: With her hand … waving?
BLACK: She's apologising.
INGRID: Saying goodbye.
COLONEL: Tata then.
SOLICITOR: Down she goes.
INGRID: Just a hand going under … a cold, dead, guilty hand.
BLACK: And she's dead.
COLONEL: And that as they say …
BLACK: … is that.

They all move away from the window. Suddenly MARGARET *slaps against the window and slides down.* ALL *on stage scream.*

Finally she is gone. ALL *sigh.*

Well, how long before the causeway lowers?

COLONEL: It should be passable by morning, Detective.

BLACK: Very well. I suggest we get comfortable. Let's all sit and give thanks to the parson for our new-found riches. It appears our murdering medico got what she deserved playing this deadly game.

SOLICITOR: Game?

BLACK: Precisely. The deadly game of …

ALL: A MIDNIGHT MURDER … AT HAMLINGTON HALL!!

COLONEL: … Hamlington Hall.

All freeze on stage. The picture (or something) falls off the wall.

There is a slight pause …

SHANE: [*quietly*] Blackout.

Blackout.

Music comes back in.

Applause.

Lights come up and SHANE *and* PHILLIPA *are kissing. Everyone is congratulating themselves.*

After a moment RICHARD *shushes the audience. The music lowers.*

RICHARD: Umm, hello. Look I probably should have mentioned this earlier. But I'm actually Councillor Richard Greenwood. And I just wanted to say … that was perhaps the worst play I've ever experienced … but, the best night in the theatre I've ever had. So … about the funding …

He gives two thumbs up.

So if you could do it exactly the same tomorrow night.

Some loud party music kicks in from next door.

Our players all congratulate each other and bow.

They did it!!

Blackout.

THE END